FEASTS
of
WINE
and
FOOD

WILLIAM MORROW
and Company, Inc.
New York

FEASTS
of
WINE
and
FOOD

WILLIAM RICE

Photography RUDY MULLER

Acknowledgments

Barbara Goldman, one of the best cooks I know, was instrumental in conceiving the menus in this book and developing the recipes for them. The inventiveness, personal style and unfailing good taste she displays when entertaining in her own home have been projected onto these pages. A keen judge of wine as well, she offered insights into matching wine with food that are reflected in the text and menus. I could not have done this book without her. Tonya Bolden Davis contributed intelligent and helpful criticism and showed extraordinary diligence in researching material for the book and transcribing the recipes. Special thanks also to Nelta Brunson, Jill Van Cleave and James Goldman.

WILLIAM RICE

Project editor for the Publisher: NARCISSE CHAMBERLAIN
Art director/Designer: ALVIN GROSSMAN
Recipes: BARBARA GOLDMAN
Food stylist: ANDREA B. SWENSON
Stylists: YVONNE McHARG and HAL WALTER

The generous assistance of Drummond C. Bell, John Hoyt Stookey, John D. Lethbridge, Richard A. Tilghman, Ron Siletto, Faith Greaves, and Arden Davis Melick is gratefully acknowledged.

Library of Congress Cataloging-in-Publication Data

Rice, William, 1938–
    Feasts of wine and food.

    Includes indexes.
    1. Cookery.   2. Dinners and dining.   3. Menus.
4. Wine and wine making.   I. Title.
TX652.R533   1987   641.5   86-23870
ISBN 0-688-06275-X

Printed in Hong Kong by South China Printing Co.

First Edition

1 2 3 4 5 6 7 8 9 10

CONTENTS

FOREWORD

When I was asked to write this foreword, I tried to think of those foods that should have no association with wine. There really are none. From the first hors-d'oeuvre to the last dessert, good wine is the ultimate complement to an elegant meal, and to a simple one as well.

Today, furthermore, no book of food and wine could be written that does not take California wines as seriously as imported wines, which were, years ago, the only "fine" wines Americans knew. The small vineyards of nineteenth-century California have grown to vast acreages that sweep across the landscape of the state, and it is California that has been the biggest single influence in enlarging the audience for wine throughout the United States.

Charles Lefranc, a Frenchman who founded California's oldest winery, Almaden, almost 135 years ago, was the first vintner to graft European grapes onto American rootstocks. Most important, he was one of the first to make wine out of Cabernet Sauvignon, the grape that defined California's stature in the wine world. Since his day, California has always been "wine country," and, after the setback of Prohibition, a mod-ern renaissance began that would eventually lead to the wine boom of the 1970s. Among the most influential early leaders was another Frenchman, Louis Benoist, also president of Almaden. He had with him a prestigious winemaker, Oliver Goulet, and as winery consultant the venerated wine writer Frank Schoonmaker, with whom he laid the foundations of the pre-eminent Almaden company of today.

Now the vintners of California are virtually innumerable, producing everything from extraordinarily fine vintages to top-quality, affordable "everyday" wines—some 65 percent of all the wine drunk in the United States. Small wonder, then, that William Rice so freely recommends California wines along with imported ones in his book on the pairing of wine and food. And he explores the possibilities and gives advice on choosing wines with a fresh and forthright point of view—that a little knowledge goes a long way and that to be an intelligent wine lover is first of all a matter of paying attention to how much you enjoy the wines you choose.

Bon appétit!

—Wayne Rogers

INTRODUCTION

WHY WINE?

Why drink wine? Why serve wine to company? Because wine is special. Wine is a magic potion with the power to make the ordinary extraordinary and the mundane pleasurable.

In the vocabulary of today, wine is an enhancer. It can make a sandwich or a piece of cheese exciting, calm frayed nerves, or become a weapon of seduction. Like nothing else, except possibly flowers, it excites the eye, the nose, and triggers the latent touch of the poet within us all. And you can't drink flowers.

Wine is not necessary to life, but very few worthwhile lifetimes or cultures, from the Sumerians onward, have been without it. The Greeks argued about the merits of imported and domestic wine. The Romans cooked it in lead pots and drank so much of it that they developed lead poisoning. Early wine salesmen went to call on the Visigoths and the Vikings. Religions, Egyptian and Christian among them, made wine a symbol of worship. Monks and hermits planted grapes and advanced wine technology, as have aristocrats and self-made millionaires in our time. Vineyards and the wine trade have survived natural disasters and government edicts. (China invoked prohibition almost 3,500 years before the United States tried it in the 1920s, with an equal lack of success.)

Why has wine been so much a part of history and art through the ages? Because wine is fascinating, a living liquid from a natural source that brings pleasure, glamour and a sense of civilized well-being whenever it is invited to share in a meal. At the simplest level, wine is pretty—sexy even—and it's fun. It makes you feel good.

To go back to the beginning, wine is created by allowing grape juice to ferment. That means it is an alcoholic beverage, like beer or whiskey, but different. There is more romance in the creation of wine, a teasing unpredictability in its taste, and unparalleled variety. Wine's different regions and types, various shades of color and hues, endless styles and vintages attract people up and down the social scale and all around the world. No one needs a degree or pedigree to enjoy drinking wine or to sense when it is good.

You may want to join the circle of wine hobbyists. It's open to anyone, male or female, young or old, who has the money and time to buy and sample a broad spectrum of wine. Serious wine tasting can lead you to new levels of knowledge, new friends and offbeat travel destinations. But you don't have to join anything. It's easy these days to find, or be directed to, a wine that will please you in a price range that is comfortable.

Improved technology, transportation and storage have provided Americans with an unprecedented selection of wine from all around the world and made "bad" wine (in the sense of wine that has spoiled) as rare as moldy bread on a supermarket shelf. That wines are so many and so different one from another is an opportunity, not a threat.

A harder task by far than finding a wine you like is to realize that taking wine casually is not a failing, that you should adjust your level of concern about serving wine to the importance of the meal and the mood of the moment. If the wine you serve brings pleasure to you and those you share it with, then you have chosen the right wine. The expert's "right" wine, famous and costly though it may be, could well be the wrong one for you, your company and the food you are serving.

The Italian peasant drinks wine because it is accessible, cheap and better than anything else he can find as an accompaniment to his daily soup, bread and pasta. He knows what a number of Americans have been discovering: When the wine chosen is appropriate to the moment and the meal, it will succeed in winning smiles and warming hearts. That is the intent of these feasts of wine and food.

A WORLD of WINE

Chapter One

Wine is found this whole world over, and a remarkable diversity of wines is available to Americans of even modest means. Kings of ages past had neither the selection nor the consistent quality we enjoy. The science of wine is highly advanced and these days is shared virtually worldwide. But all too often, the net effect of this on consumers is confusion rather than joy and eager curiosity. Like children visiting Santa at a toy store, new wine buyers can be overwhelmed by the choices.

In this book, therefore, a fair number of the world's wine will go unmentioned. There are encyclopedias that name them and wine merchants with encyclopedic selections. Seek them out when curiosity gets the best of you, which it may soon do.

Meanwhile, the purpose here is not a total wine education, but rather to present a series of feasts of wine and food that provide inspiration for delightful and, I hope, memorable home entertaining. These foods and wines are both widely available and well-suited to American tastes. More than 70 percent of the wine consumed in the United States is produced here (and 90 percent of that is made in California), with most of the remainder coming from Western Europe. Therefore, our recommendations will be from the vineyards of California and of France, Italy, Germany, Spain and Portugal.

With the menus you will find only general wine suggestions. Listing specific vineyards and vintages would only make your search more difficult, not easier, and suggest a precise fit that just isn't necessary or perhaps even possible. Blasphemous as it may sound, don't think too long or too hard when selecting a wine to serve with food.

The "truths" that emerge from clinical wine tastings are cloudy to begin with. When you add food to the equation, the possibilities for disagreement multiply in quantuum fashion. Among your scarfs or ties there may be one that is a perfect match for a blouse or suit and some that clash horribly. But several will do very well and will not cause a single eyebrow to be raised when you wear them. So it is with wine and food.

But that you serve wine to your guests is important. It adds to the glamour, conviviality and festive atmosphere of the meal. Exactly what you serve is far less important. In selecting a wine, your first decision should be the type and style (white or red, sweet or dry). Then consider the price. It's that simple.

One wine substitutes for another with surprising ease. You can change the vintage, type, even the color so long as you keep a balance between the density of taste, or "weight," of the wine and the food. The simple Wine Selection Chart on page 16 illustrates this principle. As for cost, no one has ever enjoyed a bottle of wine he thought overpriced. Buy within your budget, even for celebrations.

Wines that win prizes, like the physiques of over-muscled body-builders, are not for everyone. It's not just their style (these wines rarely like to share the limelight with food or even other wines). The price fame brings may be unrelated to the quality of the wine itself, and surely is disproportionate to that of another pleasing wine from the same neighborhood.

Sometimes, of course, wine is merely wet; a liquid of limited personality appropriate for quenching thirst or casually washing down food. Even then, unless it is sharp and nasty, it should not be dismissed. Better a silly "fun" wine than a beverage that is no fun at all.

Not only are most wines sold these days unspoiled, they are very attractive to look at. Clear, even brilliant, they do not suffer from the discoloration and sediment that prompted the use of opaque or colored wine glasses in earlier eras.

The quality of the wine, its smell, flavor and complexity, is determined by only a handful of factors: grape type, soil, climate, the wine maker and storage. (The older a wine, the more important the latter factor becomes.)

Wine lovers tend to be agricultural Darwinists. They believe the more a grape has to struggle to survive, the more intriguing the wine it will produce. Therefore, many of the world's most important wines are created at great effort and expense from grapes grown in poor soil on steep slopes in unkind climates. Provide unlimited sunlight and rich soil, experts maintain, and the result will be boozy, boring wine. Nevertheless, when you try a wine and like its taste, you have found the wine for you, no matter in what pew the wine priesthood has dictated that it be seated.

Wines in outsized containers, the much-maligned "jug" wines, lack the character of wine from noble grapes, but they have a place at the table and in this book. Most are generics—made from a mixture of unspecified grapes—that are agreeable to taste and possess the virtue of predictability. Try several and, as with coffee, you soon will find a brand to call your own. Rosé wine, dismissed as frivolous and inconsequential not a decade ago, has made a strong comeback in forms as varied as pink champagne and "blush" wines from California.

A lofty price generally indicates a wine of breeding that has received the best of care. But it cannot guarantee pleasure and, if the wine is young, may guarantee just the opposite. While the majority of the world's wine is drunk within a year of harvest, the relatively few vinous aristocrats—wines with long corks and hyphenated names—require a longer time to show their character and charm. Just when these late bloomers will mature, how to store them in the interval and how long to expose them to the air when open (the ritual known as "breathing") are subjects of endless speculation among wine buffs.

Not to disparage the deliberations of the experts, but you do not need a Ph.D. in wine to pair suitable wines with appropriate foods. A basic game plan is presented in the pages ahead, followed in the next chapter by practical information about serving meals with wine to guests.

Choosing the "Right" Wine

The chief hesitation most of us have in choosing a wine to serve with a meal is the conviction that there must be a right choice and that we, untutored as we are, will guess wrong. It can make us insecure enough to want to avoid wine altogether.

Some concern is normal, but don't let the mystique that surrounds wine scare you that much. Think about food. You know there are "perfect" food matches, such as peanut butter and jelly or strawberries and cream. You try them and immediately you understand, even as a kid. There are "perfect" food and wine matches, too, and it doesn't take long to learn about them either. They are the good clichés, familiar and safe combinations, such as roast chicken and Beaujolais or oysters and Chablis.

You will uncover a few more, but perfection is elusive. Simply drinking wine with your meals and paying attention to the taste sensations in your mouth will soon convince you that any number of wines can be suitable companions to a specific food. But not all wines. It's not *that* easy.

The taste of wine does vary depending on what food you serve it with. For a quick cram course, pour yourself a glass of wine and taste it with several different foods from the refrigerator, a piece of chicken, some cheese, even peanut butter. What counts, in this test, no matter if all the combinations are pleasant, is that the taste sensations will be different. The flavor of the wine will change, and the flavor of the food may, too. There *are* possibilities of discord. To avoid them, people rely on over-simplified rules such as red wine with meat and white with fish, or serve bland, anonymous wines in hope they won't be noticed.

In the long run, neither course is satisfying. Instead, try taking a step back. After a while, good cooks don't follow recipes by rote; they absorb the basics and are able to apply them to many different combinations of ingredients. They make substitutions, do variations and, with experience, can even improvise. So, for the moment, consider wine regions and labels as ingredients and think what you want to achieve with them.

With meals the overriding objective is compatability. Harmony is the key to enjoyment. To achieve it, you can easily learn about the perfect matches. Some other combinations are self-evident. If the food has a clear ethnic or regional identity, you can seek a wine from the same place. Italian wine with Italian food, almonds and sherry, red Burgundy with *coq au Chambertin*. This helps, but it's only one frame of reference.

The factor that really makes a wine and a food compatible when tasted together is their relative densities, how heavy or light the wine feels in your mouth compared to the food. Heavy wine will overwhelm light food and vice versa, no matter what its country of origin or even its color. Light and charming Beaujolais, so well matched with chicken, becomes shy and reluctant when it is served with duck.

What is "light"? What is "heavy"? Commercials, for "lite" beer as well as wine, have taught us that low alcohol means less calories and a lighter taste in the mouth. With wine, the more sugar there is in grapes when they are pressed, the higher the alcohol level when the juice becomes wine and the "bigger," "richer," "heavier" it can be.

Flavor, or the lack of it, counts, too. Just think of regular American coffee and espresso, how different they taste and what different effects they have on food. You might not want any food at all with an espresso and the same is true of some intensely flavored, high-alcohol wines.

Therefore, Soave, which is low in alcohol and flavor, is pleasing but a lightweight among wines. Cabernet Sauvignon, amply endowed with both, is a heavyweight.

Color can be a tip-off. Consider the appearance of these wines. Soave is pale, almost without color, while most Cabernets are deep ruby. Sometimes wines, especially ones that are not well made, may be light in color and high in alcohol. But in general, as with coffee or beers, darker color means more intense flavor. Compared to Soave, for example, a Chardonnay from California will have a golden blond color, signaling that it is probably higher in alcohol, more flavorful, "heavier."

With this in mind, glance at the Wine Selection Chart and refer to it again as you read the menus. The red and white wines recommended in the menus are all present in the chart, arranged in concentric circles.

Heavy reds and whites are placed in the Outside Circle. Middleweights are found in the next ring, the Middle Circle. Substitute any wine in each half-circle for another in the same grouping when you use a menu. The light wines, both whites and reds, are grouped together in the Inner Circle, indicating that they are interchangeable. (For dessert wines, a special case, see page 142.)

As to the real-life problem of finding wines to match the menu recommendations, age is the only other important consideration. But if you haven't yet earned your wine merit badge, to think too deeply about the fine points of aging is to risk bringing back all those insecurities. Consult with the wine seller, keeping these three rules of thumb in mind: Be sure a heavyweight white (Outside Circle) is at least two years old; look for an alternative if an Inner Circle red or white has passed its third birthday; and try not to serve a heavyweight red (Outside Circle) that is less than four years old.

Given this framework, the chart provides for a wide range of substitutions. If the Bordeaux you planned to serve with lamb is too young or is not available, choose a Cabernet Sauvignon from California or a Chianti Classico. All three are in the same circle. Or you can improvise. Instead of white wine with the grilled shrimp, serve a chilled light red, such as Valpolicello. It's not a faux pas; both wines are in the Inner Circle.

BEAUTIFUL BOTTLES

Wine bottles of various shapes and colors are identified with specific regions. From left to right: The stocky Burgundy bottle, with its sloping shoulders, is used for white and red wines, in this case a California Fumé Blanc and a Volnay. The tall brown "hock" bottle contains German wine from the Rhine River valley and there is California white in the equally tall green bottle. In the center, California's most distinctive "jug" wine bottle. Next, the strong, heavy bottle used for Champagne and other sparkling wines and the dignified, square-shouldered bottles most closely identified with the classic wines of Bordeaux.

Wine Selection Chart

RED

BARBARESCO • MATURE BURGUNDY
BAROLO • BRUNELLO
• CALIFORNIA CABERNET SAUVIGNON •
RHÔNE • HEAVY ZINFANDEL • BAROLO
MATURE BORDEAUX • AMARONE

LIGHT ZINFANDEL • YOUNG BURGUNDY
CALIFORNIA MERLOT
RIOJA • CHIANTI CLASSICO • CHIANTI • PINOT NOIR • BARBERA
GENERIC REDS FROM CALIFORNIA AND FRANCE • GAMAY BEAUJOLAIS
YOUNG BORDEAUX

DOLCETTO
BEAUJOLAIS
VALPOLICELLA • BARDOLINO
• NOUVEAU WINES •

• CHAMPAGNE & SPARKLING WINES •
ROSÉ • MACON BLANC • MUSCADET
PINOT GRIGIO • CALIFORNIA
CHABLIS • FRENCH VIN BLANC
SOAVE • ORVIETO
VERDICCHIO
FRASCATI

RIESLING • DRY RIESLING • FRENCH CHABLIS • POUILLY FUISSÉ
VERNACCIA DI SAN GIMIGNANO
SAUVIGNON BLANC • POUILLY FUMÉ • SANCERRE
CHENIN BLANC • FRENCH COLOMBARD • GAVI

• WHITE RHÔNE •
• CALIFORNIA CHARDONNAY •
EXPENSIVE BURGUNDY • GEWÜRTZTRAMINER

WHITE

Wine Descriptions

RED WINES

RED OUTSIDE CIRCLE

Rhône: Massive and slow maturing, these wines tend to be difficult with food. Think of them as boxer dogs and reserve them for hearty stews and strong cheeses. The best-known vineyard areas in the north of the Rhône Valley are Hermitage and Côte Rôtie, in the south Châteauneuf-du-Pape. A great deal of reasonably priced wine is sold as Côtes du Rhône, which tends to mature earlier than the famous vineyard wines.

Heavy Zinfandel: An intensely flavored wine, often 14 percent alcohol or more, it can be awkward, even unpleasant with food. **Light Zinfandel,** with 13 percent alcohol or less, is not as aggressive in style. It is well-suited to charcoal-grilled meats, especially steak or duck, or Italian-style beef dishes. Older tends to be better.

Barolo: The "king" of Italian reds, this is not a wine for spontaneous drinking. It can be unpleasant and bitter when young, but you will understand the term "big" when you try one that has aged, preferably a decade or more. The smell expands well beyond the glass and the taste lingers in your mouth forever. Pair Barolo with choice cuts of meat, grilled game or roasts, or chunks of Parmesan. It is fully equal to the intense flavors of wild mushrooms, truffles, even Gorgonzola cheese.

Brunello: Voluptuous, husky wines from Tuscany with a deep, berry flavor. They match well with traditional Tuscan meat dishes, roast game and beef steak, or Parmesan cheese. The high price some Brunellos fetch is due to limited production and very long life expectancy. Let collectors and restaurateurs vie for the top-of-the-line brand.

Barbaresco: This, like red Burgundy, is a wine of the heart rather than of the head. The vineyards are close to Barolo, but Barbaresco is a charming prince rather than a somber king. Serve it with red meat, especially game, squab or pheasant, wild mushrooms, strong cheeses.

Burgundy: Rich textured, sweeter and less tannic than Bordeaux, great Burgundy is a wine to love with all your heart. Finding one that fulfills its promise is the problem. Famous names, such as Musigny, Romanée, Chambertin, Clos-de-Vougeot, are very expensive and inconsistent. "They just don't make them the way they used to," old-timers say. But when you taste one that is fully mature—eight or ten years old—and truly great, you will remember it forever. Unlike white Burgundy, the reds do not match well with refined foods. Take a hint from the stocky, slope-shouldered bottle, and serve it with roast game birds, a beef stew, a pepper steak or flavorful cheeses. When **Young Burgundy** from the vineyards around Beaune is not as thin as a fashion model, it can be precociously pleasing served lightly chilled with meat pies, pâté, grilled chicken or squab, salmon or swordfish and most cheeses.

Bordeaux (called "claret" by the English): These are elegant, straight-backed, well-mannered French classics—the world's leading designer-label wines—and they come in handsome, square-shouldered bottles. They will pucker your lips when young, but gradually become more complex and intriguing as they age and should be mature in eight to ten years. There are widely publicized pecking orders for these wines, classifications that usually indicate comparative prices as well. The various châteaux have obvious stylistic differences, just like the Paris fashion houses. Shop around until you find a château that pleases you and buy a case. Bordeaux wines are well suited to rich

foods, duck, sweetbreads, liver, meats with mushroom or cream sauces, and fatty cheeses. Bordeaux and lamb is a classic combination. **Young Bordeaux:** Those labeled St. Emilion tend to be the most pleasing great Bordeaux to drink young, and even they should have three or four years of age.

Cabernet Sauvignon: California's most prestigious red wine, made from the principal grape used in Bordeaux. But the differences are as pronounced as the differences in the French and California life-styles. California cabernets tend to be big, outgoing wines that lack the discipline, patience and restraint of Bordeaux clarets. Drink them with something they won't overwhelm, flavorful foods, such as grilled duck, lamb with garlic, beef with pepper. Some of the best are expensive, limited-production collectors' items.

Amarone: Not widely known, but an ace-in-the-hole that consistently does for Italian foods what Burgundy is supposed to do for French. Full-bodied and hearty, it is ideal for rich stews, game, innards or old-fashioned pasta dishes with meat or game sauces.

RED MIDDLE CIRCLE

California Merlot: Another important Bordeaux grape, made into wine in this country without blending in juice from other grapes. It has an easy charm, but can be big and soft like an overweight football player. It is best served with grilled meats or meat and fruit combinations.

Rioja: The best-known source of Spanish red wines, the style of this region was established by immigrant French wine makers. The wines can be warm and enchanting, or as hard and distant as a bullfighter entering the ring. Best with meats served with dark, rich sauces.

Chianti Classico: As much the Italian aristocrat as Bordeaux is the French. Refined, restrained and undervalued, they are ideal companions to simply cooked meats—veal chops, game birds or a steak, for instance. A good cheese wine, too. **Chianti,** a coarser, less complex wine from the same region (Tuscany) is earthy, almost chewy. Unlike Chianti Classico, no one dresses up to drink it. Chianti won't be overwhelmed by a tomato sauce or even a barbecue sauce.

Pinot Noir: It is a forceful wine with hints of the scented pleasures of red Burgundy, but rarely—so far—the full allure. Best with meats, especially duck and beef, and cheeses.

PRODUCE OF FRANCE

VIN DU BEAUJOLAIS

CHATEAU DES LABOURONS
FLEURIE
APPELLATION FLEURIE CONTROLÉE
Red Table Wine

COMTE B. DE LESCURE
PROPRIÉTAIRE-RÉCOLTANT A FLEURIE (RHONE)
MIS EN BOUTEILLES AU CHATEAU

Alc. 13% by vol.   **IMPORTED BY**   750 ML

A L M A D E N   I M P O R T S
SAN JOSE   CALIFORNIA
SOLE AGENTS FOR THE   UNITED STATES OF AMERICA

Charles Lefranc

1981
Cabernet Sauvignon
of Monterey County

PRODUCED AND BOTTLED BY
Charles Lefranc Cellars
SAN JOSE, CALIFORNIA, BW145. ALCOHOL 12.5% BY VOLUME

C33233

Barbera: A scrappy but likable Italian kid that is being groomed to move up in class. It's smoother than Chianti these days, a nice choice for backyard steak or hamburgers from the grill, or old-fashioned chicken and veal dishes with tomato sauce.

Generic Reds from California/France: They are what they are, very useful, sound wines, made from the juice of several different grapes blended together. They bear names such as Mountain red or white, California claret or burgundy. They go with pizza, foods from the grill, sandwiches; they keep well and are very economical. Buy them to drink on a daily basis or when you have a group coming for a relaxed party. Don't hesitate to use them in cooking.

Gamay Beaujolais: California produces a wine with the Gamay grape that is stronger and less easy-going than French Beaujolais, closer in taste to a young Burgundy.

RED INNER CIRCLE

Dolcetto: Think sweet, as in nice, and you'll understand the spirit of this easy-to-drink wine. It's an Italian Beaujolais, well-suited to antipasto courses, picnic fare, in fact, anything that suits your fancy.

Beaujolais: A French wine to treasure the way you treasure a favorite pet. Keep it around and it will be loyal and undemanding, do almost anything you ask of it, and give you great pleasure. This is an ideal red wine for beginners because it is so pleasant to taste. Serve it, chilled, with almost any food, hot or cold, that isn't expensive or prepared in an elaborate way; with a roast beef sandwich but not with a standing rib roast for example. Beaujolais gets on very well with roast chicken, pork (especially sausages), pâté, goat cheeses, composed salads, even cold fish. Try serving several different types at a wine and cheese party.

Valpolicella and **Bardolino:** It may not be so in Italy, but these light, pleasant red wines are Tweedledum and Tweedledee for American consumers. Despite their color, treat them like generic white wines. Serve them chilled to drink as a cocktail, with finger foods or with first courses.

Nouveau Wines: Very young wines, produced and marketed soon after each year's harvest. They can be fun to taste, but don't count on consistent quality or buy a large supply. They should be served, well chilled, as seasonal conversation pieces. Beaujolais nouveau is the most famous, but nouveau wines are also produced in California, Italy and other regions of France.

MOSEL·SAAR·RUWER

WEINGUT GRANS-FASSIAN

LEIWEN AN DER MOSEL

>ERZEUGERABFÜLLUNG<

1984er Piesporter Goldtröpfchen

Riesling

Qualitätswein b. A. — Amtliche Prüfungsnummer 3 529 042 5 85

PRODUCE OF GERMANY   750 ml e

Weinbergsbesitz in den besten Lagen von Leiwen, Trittenheim, Piesport, Klüsserath, Dhron · Weinbau seit Jahrhunderten in der Familie

WHITE WINES

WHITE OUTSIDE CIRCLE

White Rhône: Complex, long-lived wines often high in alcohol. They go best with full-flavored fish and poultry stews, cold meats and full-flavored cheeses.

California Chardonnay: The most prestigious white wine produced in this country, now widely available. It pairs well with richly sauced poultry and fish dishes and the multiple-ingredient main-course salads that are such an important element of California cuisine. Successful chardonnays are being produced in limited quantity in other states as well.

Expensive Burgundy: Beautiful, warm and memorable, these are what most white wines would like to grow up to be. Made from the chardonnay grape, the best come from the Côte d'Or region, cost $15 or more per bottle in retail shops, have names such as Montrachet and Meursault and are bound to make you look good when you serve them. They are far too refined to upstage food and taste quite wonderful on their own.

Gewürztraminer: This wine has a spicy smell and flavor, more pronounced when produced in the Alsace region of France than in California, the two chief production areas. At their best, they will complement fatty, salty foods (including Oriental dishes) and smoked fish and meat. At their worst they are overly flowery and taste like toothpaste. Dessert wines made from sweet, late-picked Gewürztraminer grapes can be memorable.

WHITE MIDDLE CIRCLE

Riesling: These are delicious, delicate, sweet and semi-sweet wines that are much less cloying and much more useful with food than is generally supposed. Their reputation as wines to drink on their own as apéritifs is well established and well deserved. But don't hesitate to serve all but the sweetest, identified as Berrenauslese (B.A.) and Trockenberrenauslese (T.B.A.), with vegetables and vegetable soups, smoked meats, hot or cold pork and fatty fish such as herring and tuna. The B.A. and T.B.A. wines are rare and should be treated with great respect. A little goes a long way, so buy the best you can afford. Serve the wine at the end of a meal by itself or with a light fruit dessert so its special qualities won't be masked.

Dry Riesling: Wines made by vinifying the grape juice until very little residual sugar is left. The best dry Rieslings are made in Alsace and California. They go best

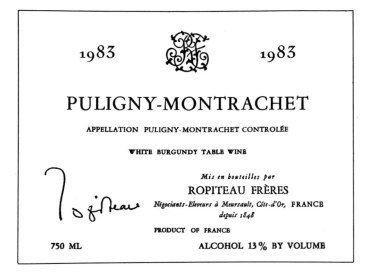

with smoked fish, fish or chicken with cream sauces and elegant picnic fare.

French Chablis: A chardonnay wine from northwest Burgundy and a famous name that fell from popularity. The region's vineyards have been revitalized and much more wine has been coming from Chablis in recent years at more reasonable prices. Chablis also is the name given to generic wine from California that is often sold in half-liter or liter containers. These wines are for everyday drinking (and cooking) and do not pretend to possess the finesse or flavor nuances of French Chablis.

Pouilly Fuissé: A chardonnay wine from France's Beaujolais region that was popularized and priced beyond its true worth. Prices have come down, but often you will find Macon Blanc a suitable substitute at a considerably lower price.

Sauvignon Blanc: This California favorite has become very popular because it is easy to drink and less expensive than Chardonnay. Sauvignon Blanc also is much less voluptuous than Chardonnay. It's a sunny-day wine to serve, well chilled, with summer foods—cold fish, fish or poultry salads, fancy sandwiches. The wine often has a distinctive smell, like cut grass or herbs. It's

unpleasant at first, but grows on you. **Fumé Blanc** is Sauvignon Blanc (or a blend featuring Sauvignon Blanc) with a catchy name created to enhance the wine's appeal to consumers.

Pouilly Fumé and **Sancerre:** These two wines are made from the sauvignon grape in the Loire region of France. Pouilly Fumé has more character, a pronounced smoky taste that couples very attractively with smoked fish, such as trout or eel, smoked chicken, and mousses, terrines or main-course soufflés containing smoked fish. **Sancerre** is as elegant and noncommital as a diplomat. Serve it before a meal to special company, with cream soups, a vegetable terrine or cold poached fish or poultry. Like the Sauvignons of California, Sancerre is a great summer wine that enhances outdoor dining.

Vernaccia di San Gimignano: A full-bodied and sturdy country wine from Tuscany. Use it when you are serving pastas, soups, stews or main-course salads that have flavorings too pronounced (herbs, olive oil or garlic) for a Soave.

Dry Chenin Blanc: The chenin blanc is a chameleon-like grape that produces sweet, dry or sparkling wines.

"Dry" Chenin Blanc is actually slightly sweet-tasting and, therefore, very pleasing to sip on its own. This hint of sweetness makes it a good companion to pork, salads containing ham or avocado, corn dishes and Oriental foods. It's not a wine to take your hat off to, or to remember for very long.

French Colombard: Think of French Colombard as a friendly cost-cutting wine. It's pale colored, somewhat tart to taste and has a faint perfume smell. Serve it in place of a more expensive white with vegetable-heavy salads, cold chicken or hot or cold shrimp dishes.

Gavi: Another of those slim-hipped, dry Italian whites, but with more pronounced smell and taste than Pinot Grigio. The step up in its cost is more than its step up in class, however, so reserve it for an occasion where the label matters. It goes well with almost any Italian seafood first course, including seafood risotto, with croquettes or even *crostini.*

WHITE INNER CIRCLE

Champagne: Very nearly the all-purpose wine. It's value at festive occasions is well known, but it is also ideal to serve before a meal and with almost any food except beef or cheeses. It is also a fine choice with highly spiced foods and Oriental cuisines. Most Champagnes are graded, according to sweetness, from "nature" (meaning no added sugar) to "demi-sec" (fairly sweet). Those in the "brut" (barely sweetened) category are the most versatile. Vintage Champagnes are considerably more expensive than non-vintage and should be purchased only for special occasions.

Rosé: Not so long ago rosé wines were thought to be merely pretty and frivolous, something to sip on Riviera terraces. But they have become much more popular lately for cocktail drinking in this country and have found a role with meals as well. California rosés, sometimes called "blush" wines, are useful as the uni-sex partners to the multi-flavored, multi-ingredient dishes California chefs are turning out. Despite their color, or lack of it, think of them as red wine that should be served cold. They are muscular enough to pair with cold red meat or highly spiced foods. White Zinfandel, Rosé of Cabernet Sauvignon, Grenache Rosé are names to look for.

French rosés from Anjou or Tavel are more delicate and can be very attractive as first-course wines, with melon and ham for example. Pink or rosé champagnes

are beautiful, romantic wines. Buy the best and save it for a special occasion.

Macon Blanc: This is a less elegant, far less expensive version of white Burgundy. It's a perfect picnic or patio wine, very useful whenever you want to serve something cool and white that has more style and character than a carafe wine. Taste several to find one you really like and then stick with the label.

Muscadet: This is a moderately priced sipping wine, the French equivalent of Pinot Grigio. Drink it with raw or cooked shellfish (other than lobster, which is hopelessly in love with white Burgundy), with fish soups or stews. In France, Muscadet with oysters on the half shell is a ritual combination. Pay attention to vintage, as Muscadet can be unpleasantly thin and acid in off years.

Pinot Grigio: Think of Pinot Grigio as an all-purpose white to serve with Italian foods. It's accessible, giving, moderately priced and widely available. It has some style, but isn't a wine serious enough to put on a pedestal and has the versatility to accompany fancy dishes (cold poached fish, for example) or something as simple as pimientos and anchovies. It's also refreshing to

drink well chilled before a meal. Try different brands until you find one that suits you.

California Chablis/French Vin Blanc: These are sound, useful wines as long as you don't try to make them into something special. They don't belong in crystal glasses or on the table with fancy-looking food. Their proper role is as a cocktail wine, in spritzers, with a snack or on a picnic. They are well matched with ham and cold meat or fish salads and sandwiches.

Soave: Don't think about Soave any longer than it takes you to say the name. Great quantities of this ultimate carafe wine come from Romeo and Juliet's hometown of Verona, where it is drunk by itself or with any food that tradition hasn't tied to red wine. A few Soaves, made by small producers, are delicate, fresh-tasting and rather special.

Orvieto, Verdicchio, Frascati: Only by the postmarks (they come from three different regions) will you be able to make any significant distinction among these wines. Serve them interchangeably, chill them well and don't hesitate to drink instead of sip them. They are light, cooling and infinitely better choices than water to quench thirst or to drink with food.

SHERRY

When you think about sherry, think of Spain: Leathery faces, hot sun, flamenco music, haunting flavors that you will find nowhere else. So it is with sherry, a beautiful, brown-hued wine strengthened by the addition of brandy and made complex by its unique aging process. Sherry is produced in this country as well as in Spain. Its depth of flavor and relatively high alcohol content make it ideal for sipping either before or after a meal. Sherries are made both dry and sweet. Dry sherries, including Amontillado and "cocktail" sherries, are well suited to teatime or for use as apéritifs. The special glasses designed for serving this wine are a luxury, but as sherry is best served chilled and in small amounts, and has a seductive aroma, their size and shape is ideal. These glasses also are of a scale that matches well with the accouterments of a tea service.

The "perfect" companion to dry sherry is also the simplest: almonds, either plain or toasted. Olives are appropriate, too, as a before-meal nibble. At table, sherry makes a good partner to consommé, cured ham, smoked fish, and highly flavored egg dishes, such as *pipérade.* The sweetest type, called Olorosso, is very sweet indeed and will be too sugary for any but the richest cakes and cookies. Here, too, an almond flavor is very compatible.

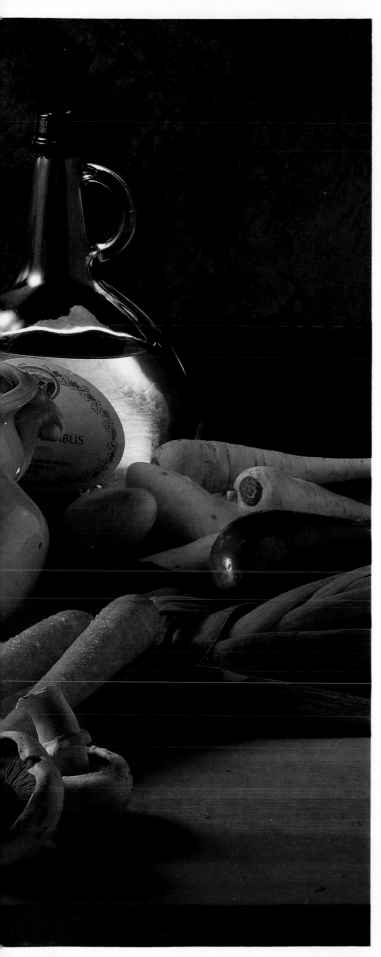

PREPARING
for a
FEAST

Chapter Two

I've learned through experience that I do myself a favor by serving wine with meals. The very fact that wine, or a succession of wines, is being poured announces to my guests that this will not be an ordinary meal. Wine glasses on the table trigger pleasant expectations—to the point, I freely admit, that, when dining away from home, I anticipate the worst when I look at a dining table and see only water glasses. Like a superb conversationalist, wine possesses the charm to bring a group gathered around a table to life. It erases tension and stimulates the mind. John Gay stated my case poetically in *The Beggar's Opera.*

> Fill ev'ry glass, for wine inspires us
> And fires us
> With courage, love and joy.

The meals in this book are blueprints for turning lunch, dinner—or even breakfast—with company into memorable occasions. They are real. The recipes have been made, the wines poured and guests have been well pleased. They are "feasts," not in the baroque sense of a vast number and vast amounts of food, but because the presentation of several courses, each with its own wine, becomes, in the dictionary's fine phrase, "a sumptuous repast."

Pouring several wines at a meal makes the event more singular, more fascinating and shows you to be a generous host. It also peps up the meal itself. Not because dinner becomes a bacchanal (you and your guests probably will consume no more than if a single wine were served all evening long), but because the distinctive personalities of the various wines make each course more interesting and more fun.

Nonetheless, your enthusiasm should be tempered by the realization that this represents a different way of dining. Europeans grow up with wine on the table during meals; Americans do not. If neither you nor your guests are accustomed to meals with wine, start cautiously. A single wine, as you probably have discovered already, is unlikely to overwhelm anyone, and if some of your guests choose not to drink or do no more than take a ceremonial sip, nothing has been lost.

But when you sense real interest and a willingness to expand horizons, when you have invited people who share your enthusiasm, a meal with a succession of wines can be as rewarding as a concert featuring music by a variety of composers. And much less complicated to orchestrate. I find only a few basic procedures and props are necessary.

The Essentials of Serving Wine

First, let's open and serve a wine, then consider the props, or accessories, and setting the table for a wine and food feast.

THE WINE

The wine you serve may be purchased for the occasion or may come from the supply of wine you have on hand. Once you begin entertaining with wine, it becomes more and more tempting to store at least a small selection at home. It's convenient. You don't have to make a special trip and having wine on hand may trigger spontaneous invitations to have friends join you for a meal. It's economical. Buying wine in quantity can cost less.

The problem, you have probably been told, is that you need a wine cellar or your investment is in danger of going over the hill and becoming undrinkable. Don't believe it. This is an extension of the philosophy that the "best" wines are the ones that take the longest to mature. For long life, 10 or 20 or more years, wine does need darkness, quiet, humidity and constant, cool temperature. If you are bitten by the collector's bug, storage space that provides such an environment becomes a consideration. For short-term storage, meaning several months or even a year, any space that's not next to a radiator or furnace or exposed to freezing cold will do. Your wine, be it a generic in jugs or from a French château, will survive very well in a closet or stashed under a staircase.

TEMPERATURE

We Americans grow up with chilled beverages. We like them with meals. That's fine for white wine. It is served chilled in restaurants. We don't hesitate to refrigerate it at home. But red wine, we are told, must be served at "room temperature." In fact, even the finest reds will be more pleasant to drink if they are considerably cooler than that. You shouldn't hesitate to put a red wine in an ice bucket or the refrigerator or near a partially opened window in cold weather, until the bottle feels chilled, not cold, to the touch. Allow 5 minutes in an ice bucket, 20 minutes in the refrigerator. Even if the wine does become overchilled, it will warm up quickly in the glass. All you need to keep in mind is a single basic equation: The simpler (less expensive) any wine is, the more it will benefit from chilling.

OPENING

Unless the wine comes in a bottle with a screw top, you will need a corkscrew to open it. If you find a jam-like substance (wine that has leaked through the cork and dehydrated) or dirt after you have cut away the capsule, simply wipe it away with a damp paper towel or a cloth. Corkscrews come in many shapes and sizes. If you've had no difficulty removing corks with the one you have, stick with it. But a succession of torn or broken corks isn't bad luck. The cause is an inferior corkscrew. Buy a new one, preferably the long, Teflon-coated style that is now widely available and seems equal to any challenge. (See page 151 for more detail on corkscrews and problem corks.)

Personally, I prefer to open wine before the meal. The process can be messy and surprisingly time consuming. Once open, the wine can be placed on a sideboard or partially recorked (you may have to turn the cork and insert the dry end) and returned to the refrigerator. Opening bottles before company arrives also allows you to pour a small taste of the wine. There is no need to offer a tasting sample at the table, as is done in restaurants—it's your wine after all; but reassuring yourself ahead of time will remove any anxiety you may have about it.

Wine snobs have a field day telling the uninitiated that wine must "breathe" and dictating a specific number of minutes or hours that should elapse between opening the wine and pouring it. But it's anybody's guess just how much time is ideal for various types of wine at various ages, and it's a game you don't have to play. If a young red seems especially harsh and characterless on sampling, you may want to pour it into a pitcher or decanter as exposure to that much air should make it taste softer and fresher.

Opening Champagne requires special attention because the trapped gas that gives the wine its bubbles is also a potential rocket launcher for the cork. Open the wine only after it is chilled and keep the cork pointed away from everyone including yourself as you remove the wire safety net. Grasp the cork and turn the *bottle* to ease the cork out without a loud pop or whoosh of fizz. Open the wine at the last moment only for ceremonial purposes. Champagne is among the hardiest of wines, and the bubbles will stay alive for a long time.

POURING

Sometimes waiters in restaurants just fill the glass. You can, too. But, depending on the size of the glass and the type of wine, you may want to be more restrained, because pouring is the key to controlling portions and assuring a fair distribution. The act of pouring is just a matter of getting the bottle over the glass and allowing the force of gravity to work. To stop the pour and forestall the possibility of allowing wine, especially red wine, to drop onto a lovely tablecloth, give the bottle a quarter-turn with your wrist as you lift it from the glass. (For disbelievers and the chronically nervous, there are special spouts sold that prevent drips.)

The real question at this point is how much to pour. Four ounces is considered a normal portion, yet no one wants to bring a measuring cup to the table. Instead, a little practice and using the same size glasses will soon give you the knack. If the glasses are the all-purpose 8 1/2- or 9 1/2-ounce size, you can fill six each about halfway from a single bottle. Fill smaller glasses higher and outsized glasses lower. The portion should be the constant in the equation. Once you've mastered this parlor trick, it's easy to calculate how many bottles you need to go around a table. Incidently, despite their various shapes, all "bottle" size containers of wine hold virtually the same amount.

There is a complex, outmoded pattern for pouring wine at a table occupied by both women and men. In this era of social equality, however, it is permissible and much more efficient to just move from one place to the next around the table.

If possible, pour the wine before each course is served. This provides continuity for the thirsty, allows your guests to taste the wine on its own and prevents the anguished looks you see in restaurants when a course is half-finished and the wine has not yet arrived. If you are acting as cook or server, it will help the wine and the party to flow more smoothly if you delegate the task of pouring wine to someone else.

The rite that sometimes occurs before the pouring stage is known as decanting. Probably you have seen photos or paintings of a wine steward peering intently through the neck of a bottle at a lighted candle as he pours wine into a decanter. That's decanting. But so is the act of pouring jug wine into a pitcher or carafe. The process becomes tricky only with older wines that have developed sediment (red wine) or crystal deposits (usually white wine). These solids emerge as part of the aging process. They are not harmful, but if not separated out, they will cloud the wine and, like sand, may cause an unpleasant, gritty sensation when the wine is drunk. Decanting is totally unnecessary with most wines. Do it to transfer jug wines into a prettier container or one of more convenient size, or to upgrade the wine by presenting it in a decanter, or, as noted before, to help make a young red more pleasing to drink.

TASTING

As with most beverages, wine is usually drunk after taking a bite of food. If you want to make some judgments about a wine, however, it is useful to smell it and take a sip before you attack the food. Swish the wine around, feel how it reacts on your tongue and various taste buds. Swallow. Breathe. The additional information on page 136, technical books and wine educators can help explain what you are sensing. For our purposes, it is enough to notice whether the taste sensations are fruity or tart and whether the flavor lingers or disappears almost immediately. The aftertaste, one hopes an agreeable one, is what wine tasters call "finish."

GLASSWARE

After the corkscrew has done its work, glasses become your most important wine accessory.

The fact that wine has been reaching a broad audience in this country has not escaped glassware designers and manufacturers. Attractive wine glasses of good quality are sold in specialty shops and discount stores for just about any price you care to pay. As with wine these days, it is hard to make a mistake. But avoid the extremes, glasses that hold minute amounts or are flamboyantly outsized, be sure they are not so delicate or daringly engineered that they are high risks for breakage and heft one to be sure it feels comfortable in the hand.

Currently, simple, sleek, clear glassware is favored. The highly decorated, colored wine glasses of earlier times are out of style, in part at least because today's wines are clear and bright in color and deserve to be admired with a minimum of distraction. Cut-glass stemware and the heavy tumblers you may have inherited are supposedly out, too; but not so far out that you may not use them, especially if several different wines are to be served during the meal. The fact is, old or unusual glassware can be both interesting and elegant.

The best starting point is a dozen or so inexpensive, all-purpose glasses. Let your own entertaining patterns and the types of wine you drink most often guide you from there. If serving wine with meals becomes a way of life, inevitably you will acquire more glasses of various sizes, shapes and value. For large parties, the first temptation is to rent glasses from a wine shop or caterer. Yet if you do this just a few times, you will have spent the cost of a couple of boxes of inexpensive but very serviceable wine glasses of your own.

Like a pipe smoker or camera buff, the wine enthusiast has the opportunity to acquire an almost limitless collection of accessories. None are essential, but there are several you will find very useful when entertaining. Chief among them for me are decanters (if only because wine looks so attractive in them), wine coasters (to keep bottles and drips off the tablecloth), stoppers

for Champagne (to keep leftover sparkling wine from going flat) and an ice bucket. I use a handsome ice bucket for its decorative effect and to save trips to the kitchen when serving apéritif wines before a meal. It is useful as well in the dining room to keep bottles intended to refill glasses well chilled. I always fill an ice bucket with a mix of ice and water (ice by itself will not chill the wine as quickly) and have a napkin near by to wipe water from the bottle when it is lifted from the bucket.

SETTING THE TABLE

The easiest way to introduce wine with meals is to serve a single wine. Match it to the main course and serve it then, or choose a versatile white or red from the Inner Circle of the Wine Selection Chart on page 16 and pour it with both the first and the main course. In either case, a single glass, possibly the all-purpose type, is all that is needed for each person. There should always be a glass of water, too. The people who make rules of etiquette say the wine glass goes to the right of the water glass. Water may be poured before the guests are seated, but the wine is meant to stay in its bottle or carafe until after they are in their places.

When you first serve a meal with more than one wine, or serve a meal to people who are not used to drinking more than one, it is less intimidating to have only a single wine glass at a time at each place and change glasses before each course that follows. Once you feel comfortable and your friends come to look forward to drinking several wines with a meal, you can take full advantage of the dramatic effect a table gives when each place setting has an array of sparkling glasses standing behind it.

Glasses of different sizes and shapes provide variety at a feast of wine and food, help avoid confusion as to which wine is in which glass and add a nice show-off touch. The etiquette books have diagrams showing you where to place them; but, in real life, the pattern can vary to suit your wishes, from straight-line or slant arrangements to a curve. As long as all the glasses are within easy reach and none is directly behind another, you've done it right. For convenience, I pour wines starting with the glass farthest to the right. Whether or not that glass is removed between courses is up to you and can depend on the number of glasses. If you want to take it away, it's easy to reach.

Choosing Food with Wine in Mind

Much too much is made of the difficulties of serving food suitable to wine. What is being sought is harmony, a pairing in which the food and the wine respect and enhance one another, a marriage.

The food in this book is full of flavor, full of character because it is meant to be enjoyed and to stimulate and intrigue your guests. Does that mean it is not suited to wine? No indeed. It means the wine may have to make some accommodation to the food, but that's in the nature of things anyway. Don't confuse a dinner at which wine is served with a wine-tasting dinner. At the latter, the point of the gathering is to taste the wines. They are chosen before the food and the food is subordinated to them.

Here the purpose is more sensual and more pragmatic: The enjoyment of wine and food in combination. Don't struggle too hard to determine the perfect blend of flavors in a recipe to support a great wine. If the wine in question is old, famous and expensive enough to warrant special attention, don't detract from it by trying to create a complicated dish. Strive, rather, for simplicity and put the wine on a pedestal; serve it with a surefire companion, a single cheese, perhaps, and let it be the one wine of such caliber during the meal. If the food is complex and highly flavored, so that you feel the wine will be overshadowed, don't put an expensive bottle into the ring and risk its being unappreciated. Serve a chilled white or red from the Inner Circle of the Selection Chart and treat it like any other beverage.

Of course, balance is a two-way street. You should be alert to the term "food wine," especially when California wines are being discussed. These are wines that are made to mature early and to be pleasant to drink. Their producers differentiate between them and the wines with enormous quantities of tannin, fruit or alcohol that are often admired by wine professionals but may not be pleasing when served with food.

Vintage, another subject of great interest to the trade and wine collectors, is almost irrelevant to our concerns. "Vintage" is, in fact, a much misunderstood word. Vintage, or *vendange* in French, is the period of time when the grapes are picked and the wine making process begins. A vintage year is a birth or graduation date, and people make the same educated guesses in wineries that they make in kindergartens or on college campuses: "It looks as though the class of '85 will turn out well," or "the class of '86 lacks promise." With wine, weather is the most important variable that causes the vintage to be classified "great," "good," "average" or "poor." Wine collectors care mostly about the two extremes, great and poor. Thanks to improvements in wine technology, years when poor wines are produced are increasingly rare, and when they occur they are widely publicized. A minimum of homework will allow you to avoid them. If a salesperson tells you another wine is from an average or good year, don't hesitate. It will be well suited to food. It is the wines, especially red wines, from a great vintage that cause problems for the consumer. If the wine is young, its greatness is not a guarantee of immediate pleasure. Quite the contrary. The price of a wine from a great vintage is higher because of what it *may* taste like in 10 or 20 years. Like a thoroughbred colt, the qualities that will make it a winner are not yet apparent.

Vintage Champagnes and Ports are different. Only in years of great promise is the wine allowed to carry a vintage date. Wines so marked are extravagances best reserved for very special occasions.

Some matches of food and wine are naturals. Then there are foods, malcontents, I call them, that often clash with wine and distort its flavor. This list is not long and common sense will help steer you away from the most obvious troublemakers. A much broader range of food is essentially neutral in regard to wine. The personalities of these foods change with the ac-cessories they wear—herbs, spices, sauces.

Descriptions of neutrals, naturals and malcontents used in recipes in this book follow. Consulting them will be helpful when planning food and wine feasts of your own. To further ease any anxiety you may feel about making the "right" match, keep in mind that the careful controls of formal wine tastings go out the window when a group of people with widely differing senses of taste gather at your table to eat and drink. You cannot orchestrate the pace at which they drink, nor command that they sip only after a bite of the lamb, nor control the amount of attention they will pay to either the food or the wine.

You probably have experienced the delight of having a wine with no claim to fame suddenly taste wonderful with something you are eating. The wine has met a natural and is benefiting from the flavor and texture of the food. With neutral foods, experimentation—trying different wines with the dish—will help you find the wines that are most compatible. Experimentation also will teach you that some wines do quite well with potentially troublesome foods and seasonings. For instance, sparkling or sweet wines do well with salty foods. With highly seasoned food, try sparkling wine or slightly sweet white wines. With fruit, sweet and semisweet wines. With sweet foods, sweet and sparkling wines. Finally, our taste buds are quite resilient. Bread, or potato or rice served with assertively flavored food will set things right again.

Cooking with wine and serving sauces made with wine can help make foods more compatible with the wine you drink. See the section on Cooking with Wine, page 143.

THE NATURALS

Lamb: This is the best meat of all to serve with wine. The two support one another, no matter what the cut or the wine. Furthermore, lamb is a grown-ups' meat, served in fancy restaurants and at elegant parties. It's easy to cook and can be served in chops or slices. There are two suggestions you should heed regarding lamb: Pay whatever it takes to buy the best quality available, and cook the meat as rare as you and your guests will accept it. You cannot expect a wonderful taste experience if the lamb is dry and brown. Herbs, mustard and garlic are fine as seasonings, but when serving wine, leave the mint jelly in the cupboard.

Shellfish: Think of shellfish as meat that lives in the water and feel confident that all the species go well with wine, whether they are raw, cooked or barely cooked.

Game: Venison, boar, wild hare. In spirit these are foods of an earlier time and serving them calls to mind a less refined, more lusty style of dining. The bigger the piece you can cook, a haunch or saddle, if possible, the better. The flavor is much more pronounced than that of domestic meat, so go all out with the richest, most full-bodied wine you can find; something with an aroma you "can't keep in the glass with a fence."

Wild Mushrooms: As with game, do not confuse the wild product with the tame. When cooked, wild mushrooms radiate a vivid, earthy odor reminiscent of musk. They will stand up to and enhance the most intense, full-bodied red wine you serve. The same is true of black truffles.

Game Birds: To fully appreciate the distinctive taste of the bird, and to achieve the best harmony with wine, roast them on the rare side. Dark-meat birds, duck or squab, are happiest with rich, ripe reds. With light-meat birds, quail or pheasant, serve Middle Circle reds or Outside Circle whites.

Pork: Traditionally pork—light in color, firm textured, fatty and with a touch of sweetness—has been matched with Riesling or fruity young wines. The difficulty these days lies with the pork, not the wines. It has become much less fat, less flavorful, and becomes very dry when cooked to recommended temperatures. Roast or bake loins or racks for less time than older cookbooks direct, serve the pork with mustard or fruit-based sauces and consider ·serving a "blush" wine or Champagne with it.

Fruit: Fruits are wonderful companions for wine. They benefit from being cooked in wine, bathed in wine without cooking or merely served with it. Among the most compatible fruits are apricots and peaches.

Cakes and Cookies: They should be unfrosted and not very sweet tasting. Match this type of cake or cookie with semisweet or sweet wines. You will need nothing more to bring a wine meal to a very pleasant conclusion.

Bread: As many a picnic veteran knows, for pure, simple pleasure it is hard to beat the combination of a fresh, crusty loaf of bread and a bottle of wine. Spread some sweet butter on the bread to compensate for the frosting you omit from the cake. Bread is better than any other food at both enhancing the flavor of wine and restoring your taste buds before the next sip.

Two foods generally thought to be natural matches with wine—cheese and beef—actually need to be considered separately.

Beef: Beef is not nearly as congenial as lamb to a broad range of wines. It's a dense meat and when grilled needs a robust, full-bodied wine. Even roast beef is so rich it does not harmonize well with complex wines. A wine-based sauce with the meat can help bridge the gap. Look to reds from the Outside Circle to accompany beef braised or stewed with wine.

Cheese: "Wine and cheese" rolls off the tongue like "bread and butter," but a perfect match of wine and cheese is not that easy to find. Cheese, the dominant partner, can be very kind to wine. Sometimes, though, there are clashes that leave only an unpleasant taste in your mouth. You have to know your way around a cheese board. To begin, think about the characteristics of each type. If a cheese is pale white and virtually odorless, match it with an Inner Circle white or red. If it is rich and buttery (double- and triple-crèmes, such as Brie and Explorateur) a Middle Circle red will be a good companion. For salty blue cheeses, such as Roquefort, select a sweet wine. If the cheese is very ripe and defiantly challenges you to dare to smell it, seek out the most full-bodied Outside Circle red you can find. Also, wines and cheeses of the same country, especially the same region, tend to pair well together. When you feel confident, relegate the tray with several cheeses on it to wine-and-cheese parties and generally, at meals, select a single cheese to go with a specific wine.

THE NEUTRALS

Starches and Grains: Potatoes, noodles, rice and other grains are all useful on the menus of wine and food meals because they provide a buffer between the wine and any strong, aggressive flavors on the same plate. In a Szechuan restaurant, for example, rice will neutralize more effectively the pain caused by eating hot pepper than any liquid. When planning a menu that includes highly seasoned foods, include a bland starch or grain. You will do the wine, and your guests, a favor.

Chicken and Turkey: Chicken is the most versatile character actor in the food world. Those sold in our supermarkets are so bland they will take on even the most subtle flavors of a sauce or stuffing. How you prepare chicken, then, should determine your choice of wine. Roasted without stuffing, it is an ideal match for a chilled light red or rosé. Poached and served with a rich cream sauce, the chicken responds well to a Middle Circle white. Baked with herbs, garlic and tomatoes, chicken tastes best with a Middle Circle red. The same pattern holds true for turkey. There is an ongoing debate among wine lovers about the "right" wine to serve with Thanksgiving turkey. The problem really isn't the turkey. The stuffing, condiments and the other foods that are piled on the plate with the turkey are what make the choice difficult. I usually serve both a light, fruity red wine and a white from the Middle Circle and encourage guests to try one or both.

Finfish: The sole family is wine-friendly. So are most other firm-fleshed, white-colored fish. You can serve whatever white wine you wish with them. The elegance of the occasion, the sweetness—if any—of the sauce and the price you wish to pay should determine your choice. Despite a fad for serving chilled red wine with these fish, I find they often accentuate the tannin and make the wine taste bitter. This is not true, however, of darker meat fish, such as tuna, swordfish and salmon. With these fish, which often are cut into steaks and grilled like red meat, a chilled red or a full-flavored white is a good choice.

Vegetables: Most vegetables coexist with wine quite peaceably. Potatoes, string beans, squash, legumes, even members of the cabbage family are neutral accompaniments unless they have picked up distinctive flavors during cooking or from a sauce. Some vegetables accused of being troublemakers, spinach and asparagus, for example, cause little noticeable change in wine if cooked with butter or served with a butter sauce.

THE MALCONTENTS

Chocolate: This is one of the most overpowering, long-lasting flavors of all. When serving wine with a chocolate dessert, don't pick anything special. The quality of the wine will not show. The most successful match for chocolate is Port. Champagne works well, too, and is handy to have around if a dessert toast is in order.

Artichokes: Intensely sweet, they make wines taste bitter and sometimes metallic. Nonetheless, domestic artichokes provoke less harsh reactions from wine than those grown in Europe. A slightly sweet wine will survive quite well. So will Champagne.

Citrus Fruit: These fruits push dry wines over the edge and make them taste too tart. Orange is friendlier to wine than lemon or grapefruit, however. Sweet wines can be served with citrus fruit tarts and with other citrus fruit desserts where added sugar counteracts the acid.

Vinegar: Vinegar and wine. You might as well say Cain and Abel to a wine lover, and if the vinegar in question is from a supermarket, it will do harm to any wine it comes in contact with. But vinegar made from quality wine and used sparingly won't destroy your palate for wine. Nor will the same vinegar when cooked as part of a recipe.

Cranberry: Cranberries may be even more antagonistic to wine than vinegar. At any rate, it's a close comparison. Don't let the sugar that is added to cranberry jelly or relish mislead you. During the Thanksgiving feast, eat something else before you take a sip of wine.

Liquor: By itself, liquor is too strong and harsh to be compatible with wine, as the taste of wine and alcohol cocktails that are served in bars proves. When using liquor for a sauce, either burn off the alcohol or cook the sauce for some time after the alcohol is added.

Corn: Perhaps it is the combination of sweet and starch, but fresh corn on the cob distorts the taste of wine considerably. This is less noticeable when the corn, already cooked, is used in a cream soup or baked in a custard.

Salads and Bitter Greens: If salad is the first course, as often happens in French Riviera or California menus, don't overdo on the amount of bitter greens used, go easy on the vinegar in the dressing and don't serve a great wine. If you feel the need in your menu for a salad with a powerhouse dressing—a first-course Caesar salad or a green salad with a tart vinaigrette after the main course—there is no need to search for a suitable wine to accompany it. Omit wine with that course, and be sure there is bread available. As raw, bitter greens, such as endive, escarole, arugula and chickory, are most often used in salads and tartly dressed, they needn't come in contact with wine unless someone continues to sip wine from a previous course. When cooked, bitter greens may still be troublesome if they meet a wine without a bite of something else taken in between.

Peppers: Hot peppers are a pain, literally and figuratively. Sweet peppers, either red or green, are not so much bad guys as warning signals—often they are part of a highly seasoned dish. If it's a California-style salad or pizza, think about drinking a full-bodied California wine, or something from Italy or Spain.

Condiments: The list is long, and almost all condiments represent a threat. Be they sauces or relishes, sweet or spicy, they show wine no respect. Don't give them up, just use them judiciously and don't follow a bite of one with a sip of wine. French mustard, often made with unfermented wine juice, is an exception.

Making a Menu ❧

Entertaining with food becomes a little different once wine enters the picture. Your meals will last longer and become more convivial. But finding the food to please the company remains the prime consideration. Suitable wines will be found once the menu is set. Furthermore, given the same dishes, the wines you choose to serve can move the meal upscale or downscale, depending on how elegant or simple they are.

It's a common mistake to confuse meals with wine and wine banquets or diplomatic dinners. Blame that on the French. They made the rules for formal dining: consommé to fish to meat to salad to cheese to dessert. Wine (French, of course) was served with each course except the salad. The English were allowed a savory and a glass of Port at the end. All pomp and too few variables in the circumstances. The required style for such a meal involves formal clothes, servants, a kitchen full of cooks—and the awful fear of doing something wrong.

An occasion should be an occasion. There are times and places for dressing up and indulging in formal rituals. But wine is not a tuxedo. You can wear it every day. Wine is on hand to help, not hinder, the staging of a successful social gathering. Accept it as a friend, a tool, a helpmate and it won't let you down.

In creating the menus in the next chapter, one goal was to recognize some realities of life today in the United States: the fact that we eat less, and in less rigid menu patterns, than did earlier generations. Our passion for assertively flavored foods. The widening availability of high-quality foods and wines from around the world. The absence of domestic help in most homes. Another goal was to show what a wonderful range of situations and events are suited to becoming feasts of wine and food. You will find menus designed for family parties, informal as well as formal entertaining, meals for as few as four or up to ten guests and for at least one intimate, romantic interlude.

These menus are eclectic, multinational and filled with distinctive flavors because that is the way people like to eat these days. In deference to the wines, many of the recipes are deliberately simple, but they will show you off as a skillful, imaginative cook and host. Part of the intent of this menu collection is that individual elements can be used alone, mixed and matched with courses in other menus, and become the basis for creating feasts of your own.

You will discover that quite a few classic rules are broken in the pages ahead, that unconventional wine and food pairings are suggested. This is not intended to shock. It occurs because the matches—of courses, of wines, of food and wine together—felt natural, comfortable and were exciting to taste. For example, look at the Movie Night party on page 59. It's an informal occasion and the dinner is served informally. Clearly the wine will be a supporting player and the generic wine recommended is right for the part. The title of another menu, Homage to Chardonnay, informs everyone that wine will be the center of attention, in an all-white-wine menu.

This is not a teaching cookbook. The objective is to help you enjoy preparing and presenting meals with wine easily, gracefully, as effortlessly as possible. Another reality we face is the presence of excellent prepared foods. Buy them. Use them. You will find some convenience products and commercial ingredients listed in various recipes because they work very well and taste very good. The same is true of the generic and inexpensive varietal wines that are recommended. They belong with their menus and a more expensive wine will not necessarily make a better match.

In this era of streamlined dining, a menu of three courses, each with its own wine, is one I use frequently for a meal with company. There is nothing threatening about a meal of this size. It's similar to the old-fashioned family dinner back in the days when there were old-fashioned families. Yet the succession of plates and bottles and the variety of food and wine make the meal something special.

Some of the recipes are rich. Many are lean. In the menus, rich and lean are balanced, yet somewhere in each menu is a showpiece dish. It may be as elegant and expensive as the saddle of lamb in Dinner at Eight on page 85 or as simple and eye-catching as the giant ravioli on page 71.

When it comes to preparing these recipes, you will find a lack of culinary trickery. The cooking techniques are basic and the equipment and ingredients widely available. There is a maximum of do-ahead preparation and a minimum of irrelevant garniture and fuss. Where presentation does become time consuming, as in some nouvelle cuisine-inspired dishes, a microwave oven will be extremely useful for rewarming.

The key to success, especially with simple straightforward recipes, is to use the best quality ingredients you can find. It will be money well spent. You have a head start on achieving a triumph of flavor. You will save time and effort. Also, wine is both an excuse to invoke quality and a reward for doing so, because the wine and food pairings will focus attention on the food and the wine will make it taste better.

There are many theories on how to present a sequence of wines with a meal. The classic French pattern is to serve wines from the youngest to the oldest, and the lightest (in body) to the heaviest. With modern menus, however, it's best to just let the food in each course dictate the style and heft of the wine. Serve red before white? Why not, if you are eating a meat dish, such as the carpaccio on page 80, before grilled fish or chicken? The rules were made before all sorts of dishes, including ·California-style main-course salads and salmon- and caviar-topped designer pizza, were invented.

The menus suggest appropriate types of wine with specific courses. The Wine Selection Chart on page 16 and the wine descriptions that follow it indicate to you what these wine types are like. You then select specific wines, basing your choice on availability and how much you want to spend on them. These recommendations are suggestions, of course, not commands. Omit, or add, wines to suit your own sensibilities and consult the chart for guidance in making substitutions.

As you will see, not every course has a separate wine. Sometimes, even in a wine-oriented meal, there will be a food that, like Greta Garbo, wants to be alone. A vinegar-laced salad is the most obvious example, but you will find others. Also, if a wine is compatible with two consecutive courses, there is no need to change. Just open another bottle of the same wine and keep pouring. Sometimes it makes sense to pour only a single wine throughout the meal, or, as with the spice-accented Casual Summer Meal on page 108, to offer both a white and a red and let guests choose one or try both.

The menus suggest much more red wine than you may be used to drinking. Wine professionals seem to like red wine more than do consumers, who buy more white. But when sipped with many foods, not just meat, red wine becomes less complex in taste and is pleasing to drink, especially when served slightly chilled. In fact, re-creating these menus probably will lead you to a number of wines you may have read about and seen in wine shops but never knew quite how to use: Sweet wines, especially Rieslings from Germany and California, are wonderful companions to a variety of first courses and desserts. Champagne shouldn't be held back for birthdays and weddings only. Wines with names such as Gewürztraminer, Chenin Blanc and Zinfandel can dance like Fred Astaire with the right partners.

It is a safe rule of thumb to plan on opening a bottle of wine per person at a meal with wine. For a three-course meal, here's how it works: For a group of four, you will open a fresh bottle with each course (that's three bottles) and probably drink part of a second with the main course (that's four). With six at table, refills for each of the three courses will require a second bottle, or six in all.

This amount of wine may seem overwhelming, but I can assure you that it is not. The wine is being served with food over a period of time. You and your guests will absorb it easily, and there is no obligation to pour it all, nor for guests to empty each glass. Furthermore, you are going to be a much more relaxed host if you have too much wine instead of too little. Unused wine keeps, at least for several days. It is useful with leftovers the next day, for sipping by itself, for cooking and, all other options failing, it can become the base for terrific homemade vinegar (see page 145). When you drink wine with only one other person, rarely will you open more than a single bottle. Satisfying enough, but a single note, a single dimension. The feasts of wine and food that follow offer a different approach to meals, no matter how few or how many are sharing in the celebration.

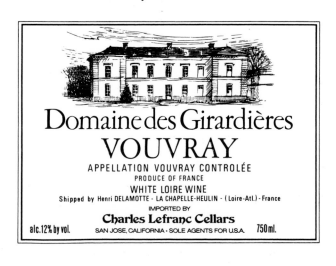

MENUS & RECIPES

Chapter Three

Before the feasts commence, it is important to contemplate the strategic questions of how you might prepare and serve them. Except for advice on orchestration, no on-going attempt has been made to order the routine to be followed in your kitchen, nor to dictate serving methods. It's far better that you establish the art of the possible for yourself and execute these menus at your own pace and present them in your own style.

But you will soon notice certain patterns that repeat themselves. The detail work is almost always at the early preparation stage and usually can be done well ahead of the meal itself. Very infrequently does a first course require more than saucing or reheating at the last minute. Rarely does a menu begin with an expensive, drop-dead wine. Rather, the multicourse meals build up to a showcase dish and wine. There is no need for a lengthy pre-meal period with apéritif refills and hors-d'oeuvre. The meal itself and its ample complement of wines is the focus of the gathering, so proceed to table as soon as is practicable after all the guests have arrived.

The facet of true sophistication that links these feasts, the humble as well as the fancy, is an assumption that you will purchase and serve the best of what you can afford, be it caviar or beautiful home-grown vegetables, in lavish amounts. Don't force second helpings on your guests, but make it clear that more is available and allow time for those who take advantage of your invitation to enjoy the food.

Ours is a deliberately casual era for entertaining. However, it is possible for casualness to descend into chaos. In planning a meal, as host or hostess, you have the opportunity to create a structure. Then let your guests know what's ahead, how many courses and how many wines will be served. The formality or informality of the table setting helps establish the mood of the gathering. Read each menu and the recipes before beginning it—not just to compile a shopping list, but to gain a sense of how you can best prep, cook and serve it. Then your imagination can go to work to make the feast your own.

Do-it-yourself is acceptable, even chic, these days and the menus are tailored for the home cook with only a single pair of hands. But it's up to you to budget enough time and reserve enough energy to be a vital part of your own party.

There is no need to pretend that dinner made itself or that you are making do on the servants' night off. For instance, there is a good deal of cooking needed to prepare the Family Gathering that opens this chapter, and even if you present it buffet style, you will want assistance in serving. But what are family for? Asking some of them to help makes sense. On the other hand, the Wine Banquet (page 74), with five courses and five wines, is planned for only six people, not the crowd the word "banquet" may connote. It's less effort than you might suppose. But here, as with the easy-to-cook Dinner at Eight menu (page 84), serving so many courses and so many wines requires careful choreography. Instead of trying to do everything yourself, enlist men at the table as waiters and sommeliers. All dressed up, with specific tasks to do, they will respond as though they were veterans of a great French restaurant. The women, meanwhile, will be twice pleased: to be waited on and to not feel obligated to help out while wearing evening clothes.

At parties, you cannot command laughter or rehearse spontaneity. But wine fuels both. It is a better cure for stiffness than Ben-Gay and an almost infallible conversational stimulant. Wine ensures that you will leave a convivial group behind while you retreat into the kitchen to finish the next course. No ominous silence will follow you. You can take your time and complete the presentation of the next course to your satisfaction, which is good for you and good for your guests. A feast of food and wine should be a leisurely event—a play with its own pace and intermissions between the acts. It's the presence of wine at the performance that makes all the difference.

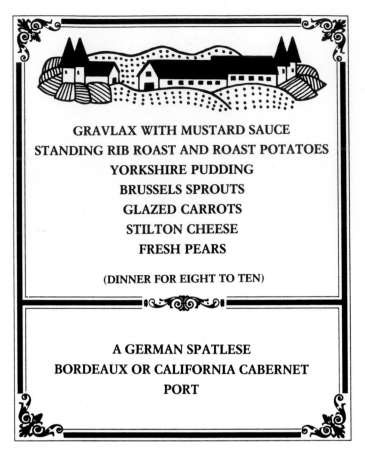

GRAVLAX WITH MUSTARD SAUCE
STANDING RIB ROAST AND ROAST POTATOES
YORKSHIRE PUDDING
BRUSSELS SPROUTS
GLAZED CARROTS
STILTON CHEESE
FRESH PEARS

(DINNER FOR EIGHT TO TEN)

A GERMAN SPATLESE
BORDEAUX OR CALIFORNIA CABERNET
PORT

FAMILY GATHERING

Rich is as rich does, and, with no apologies, this is a rich meal—expensive, beautiful, traditional, a showcase for prime ingredients. Any thought of compromise, any temptation to substitute frozen Brussels sprouts for fresh, and you should walk away from it. If you stay with it, the rewards are the sort of meal children remember always and, as adults, dream of finding again.

🍷 Begin with a lightly honeyed spatlese from the Rhinegau, just the right match for the cured salmon. The beef needs a wine of character and dignity, but leave your precious vintage or costly prize-winner in the cellar; this is too rich a course for such bottles. With your cheese, a mellow Port and some nicely sliced ripe pears. In its classic way, it becomes the icing on the meal.

🍴 Place the roast on a platter and put an adroit guest in charge of carving. Something as beautiful and impressive as a full seven-rib roast should always be carved in front of an audience.

A menu such as this is best served from a sideboard. Two people to serve are enough. The issue is keeping the food hot; a few perfect Brussels sprouts may garnish the roast platter, but otherwise the practical thing is to bring both vegetables and the roast potatoes to the dining room each in a heated covered dish. Bake the Yorkshire pudding in attractive ovenware that can be taken straight to the sideboard.

♀ The Stilton and pears should be served at room temperature. The photograph shows the traditionally approved way for Stilton to be cut and presented wrapped in a linen napkin.

GRAVLAX WITH MUSTARD SAUCE

GRAVLAX
1 cup sugar
1/2 cup coarse salt
1/2 cup coarsely ground black pepper
2 fillets from an 8- to 10-pound salmon, with skin on
3 large bunches dill, coarse stems removed
1 teaspoon olive oil
Lemon slices

Combine the sugar, salt, and pepper. Line the bottom of a very deep, glass or enameled pan with 1/2 bunch of dill. Cut the fillets in half to fit them into the pan. Lay in one piece of a fillet, flesh side up. Cover with 1/2 bunch of dill and 2/3 cup of the spice mixture. Place the matching piece of fillet on top, skin side up. Cover with 1/2 bunch of dill. Repeat the process with the remaining two pieces of salmon. Now spread the remaining dill and spice mixture over all. Cover loosely with aluminum foil and weight down with a pie dish filled with cans or pie pellets.

Refrigerate for 3 days, turning over the pairs of fillets after the first 1 1/2 days. After 3 days, remove from the pan and rinse briefly under cold water to remove the excess salt. Pat dry.

Slice the gravlax several hours before serving. Slice thinly across the grain, as you would smoked salmon. Arrange the pieces in overlapping circles on a serving platter and brush lightly with the olive oil to make them glisten. Garnish with the lemon slices. Serve with Mustard Sauce.

MUSTARD SAUCE
3 cups mayonnaise
2 tablespoons Dijon mustard
2 tablespoons grainy mustard
1 tablespoon sweet German mustard
1 tablespoon lemon juice
8 to 10 drops Tabasco sauce

Combine all the ingredients in a bowl. Adjust the seasoning to taste. The sauce should be made ahead to allow the flavors to meld.

STANDING RIB ROAST AND ROAST POTATOES

One 7-rib roast of beef
12 small baking potatoes, peeled and quartered
Salt and freshly ground black pepper to taste

The beef should be at room temperature. Roast in a 400-degree oven to an internal temperature of 120 degrees, about 1 1/2 hours for rare. Let rest for at least 20 minutes before serving.

Parboil the potatoes for 10 minutes. Drain. Ten minutes before you remove the roast, place the potatoes around the meat, baste them with the hot fat in the pan, and season them with salt and pepper. Baste the potatoes again occasionally with the fat after you have removed the roast and cook until they are crusty, about 30 minutes in all, while the roast rests.

YORKSHIRE PUDDING

2 cups all-purpose flour
1 1/2 teaspoon salt
1 cup milk
4 eggs
1 cup water
1/2 pound unsalted butter

Combine the flour, salt, and milk in a bowl. Beat in the eggs. Add the water and beat until bubbly. Refrigerate for 2 hours.

Preheat the oven at 400 degrees. Divide the butter equally between two heatproof baking dishes, about 8 by 8 by 2 inches, and place in the oven to melt. Restir the batter and divide it evenly between the baking dishes of sizzling butter. Return to the oven and bake for 20 minutes. Then reduce the oven temperature to 325 degrees and continue baking for 15 to 20 minutes, or until brown.

BRUSSELS SPROUTS

Three 10-ounce cartons fresh Brussels sprouts
12 black peppercorns
4 tablespoons unsalted butter
Salt and freshly ground black pepper to taste

Cut off the root stems and cut a cross 1/4 inch deep in the bottom of each sprout. Cook with the peppercorns in boiling water until tender but still a bit crisp, about 10 minutes. Immediately plunge into cold water; then drain.

Melt the butter in a saucepan. Turn off the heat, add the Brussels sprouts, and toss until coated. Cover, set aside, and reheat just before serving. Season with salt and pepper.

GLAZED CARROTS

2 pounds baby carrots, peeled and trimmed
1 1/2 cups chicken broth
1/2 cup dry vermouth
4 tablespoons unsalted butter, in all
2 tablespoons sugar
3 black peppercorns
Salt and freshly ground black pepper to taste

Cook the carrots in the broth, with the vermouth, 2 tablespoons of the butter, 1 tablespoon sugar, and the peppercorns until tender but still crisp, about 10 minutes. Remove the carrots, cool under running water, and drain. To the cooking liquid add the remaining 2 tablespoons of butter and the 1 tablespoon of sugar. Boil until reduced to a glaze.

To serve, reheat the carrots in the glaze and season with salt and pepper.

CUCUMBERS STUFFED WITH HAM MOUSSE
SAUTÉED VEAL MEDALLIONS
SPRING VEGETABLES
POTATO FLOWERS
FRESH FIG PRESERVES
GOAT CHEESES

(DINNER FOR EIGHT)

MACON BLANC
CALIFORNIA CHARDONNAY
EXPENSIVE WHITE BURGUNDY, SUCH AS MONTRACHET

HOMAGE TO CHARDONNAY

White wines can be as big as reds—and here is a menu to prove it. This is an elegant dinner, an homage to your guests as well as to the Chardonnay grape.

Macon is low on cost but high on flavor, plenty of it for the ham mousse. And California Chardonnay is rich, full-bodied stuff. As for white Burgundies, you haven't lived until you've had a fine one.

You will need twenty-four glasses. They do not have to be the same; three different sets work as well and provide visual clues to what wine you are drinking, which helps particularly when all the wines are white. It's nice to progress from an informal glass to more formal ones in a dinner like this, reserving your most elegant goblet for the white Burgundy.

Any small vegetable will work as garnish for the veal—asparagus tips, young green beans, miniature carrots or turnips. Parboil them until they are almost tender, drain, and set aside in a pan with a little melted butter; reheat just before serving. To serve eight and keep everything hot, rather than using a platter, you may prefer to arrange the main course on warmed dinner plates in the kitchen.

As a rule, you should nominate only one person to help you with serving and a second person to serve the wine. Having everyone pitch in is confusing and detracts from the elegance of the meal. You can remove the glasses after each course or leave them on the table.

CUCUMBERS STUFFED WITH HAM MOUSSE

3/4 pound piece of Black Forest or Westphalian ham, trimmed and cubed
1/2 cup heavy cream
1 whole egg
1 egg yolk
2 tablespoons unsalted butter
1 teaspoon lemon juice
4 drops Tabasco sauce
Freshly ground white pepper to taste
4 seedless English cucumbers
16 *cornichons* (small sour gherkins)

Place all the ingredients, except the cucumbers and the *cornichons,* in a food processor. Process until the mixture has the consistency of a smooth mousse.

Score the skins of the cucumbers, slice into 1/2-inch rings, remove the soft centers, and place the rings on a baking sheet. Pipe the mousse into the rings with a pastry bag. Cover and refrigerate until the filling is firm.

Drain the *cornichons* and cut them each lengthwise into thin equal slices, stopping just short of the bottom, then fan the slices out. When ready to serve, divide the stuffed cucumbers equally among individual plates and garnish with 2 *cornichons* in the center.

SAUTEED VEAL MEDALLIONS

8 veal medallions
6 tablespoons unsalted butter
6 tablespoons olive oil

Ask the butcher to cut the medallions about 2 inches thick from the veal tenderloin. Heat the butter and oil in a heavy skillet. Over high heat sauté the medallions, turning once, until golden brown, about 4 minutes per side.

Note: This recipe can sound scary because it is so simple. However, if you have wonderful veal, cooking it simply is the best way. You probably do not even need salt and pepper.

POTATO FLOWERS

1/2 pound unsalted butter, clarified
1 cup olive oil
10 California new white potatoes, washed, skin on
Salt and freshly ground black pepper to taste

Heat the butter with the olive oil. Using a vegetable peeler, cut the potatoes into long, paper-thin, flexible slices (1). Immediately, to prevent the potato slices from discoloring, coat them in the butter and oil mixture.

Form the "flowers" in a muffin pan: Start building eight potato flowers by laying four slices in the form of a cross in each muffin cup (2). You now have a base to start creating flowers. Curl the slices around one finger to form little cones and place in the cups, jamming them in

so they stand upright. Open some of the cones, varying their shape slightly. They *will* look like flowers (3). Sprinkle them with salt and black pepper and any extra oil and butter you have left.

Preheat the oven to 400 degrees. Bake the flowers until they are browned, about 35 minutes (4). They may drip while cooking, so place a large baking pan underneath.

Notes: This sounds hard, but once you get the hang of it, it is very easy as long as the potato slices are thin enough to be very flexible. A "mandoline" for cutting will speed up the process. Well coated with the butter and oil, the flowers can be held uncooked for about 1 1/2 hours. They don't reheat well.

(1)　　　　　**(2)**

(3)　　　　　**(4)**

FRESH FIG PRESERVES

12 fresh figs, unpeeled and rinsed
1/2 cup white wine
1 strip of lemon peel
1/2 teaspoon freshly ground black pepper
1 tablespoon sugar
1 teaspoon lemon juice

Combine all the ingredients in a saucepan and simmer for about 15 minutes. Press through a coarse sieve into a bowl. The figs may be served hot or cold with the veal; pass in a sauceboat.

GOAT CHEESES

To the extent that any cheese is chic or hot or in, goat cheese is it. French, Italian, and domestic, they are made in a variety of shapes, sizes, textures, and flavors. They vary from mild and creamy to dry and hard, all with the slightly tangy flavor of goat's milk. Get several different kinds and present them on a tray. They make a beautiful display and your white Burgundy deserves it.

CORN SOUP

CRAB BOIL

SWEET-POTATO FRIES

DEEP-DISH PEACH PIE

(LUNCH FOR EIGHT)

FRENCH COLOMBARD

CRAB-BOIL PICNIC

This meal IS a picnic—and it works in the yard or in the kitchen. Boiled crabs cannot be eaten neatly; use dish towels instead of napkins and dive in.

The tart, slightly fragrant Colombard is a nice foil for the spicy flavors of the soup and crab boil. It's an easy-to-drink thirst quencher, so skip a dessert wine.

Both the crabs and the sweet-potato fries are cooked just before serving, and you are serving eight. But this is the opposite of a problem. The cooking for a meal like this is a part of the festivity—and, anyway, the soup and the dessert are ready ahead.

CORN SOUP

Eight 16-ounce cans whole-kernel corn
1/4 pound butter
1 small onion, chopped
8 black peppercorns
2 quarts chicken broth
1 cup honey
16 drops Tabasco sauce
1 teaspoon lemon juice
2 cups milk

Drain the corn and put it in a heavy pan. Add the butter, onion, and peppercorns. Pour in the chicken broth (it should just cover the corn). Bring to a boil, partially cover, and simmer for 30 minutes.

Purée the soup in batches in a food processor or blender and pass it through a sieve, pressing hard on the solids. Return the soup to the pan, add the honey, Tabasco sauce, lemon juice, and milk. The soup should be the consistency of very heavy cream; if necessary, add more broth and/or milk. Stir well. Reheat to serve, tasting for seasoning. Serve in mugs.

CRAB BOIL

12 ounces beer
One 8-ounce box seafood boil
1 tablespoon hot red pepper flakes
32 large live blue crabs

Fill a large pot three-quarters full of water and bring to a boil. Add all the remaining ingredients and return to a boil. Cook the crabs just until they turn reddish. Drain.

To serve, cover a table with newspapers and provide wooden mallets and seafood picks.

SWEET-POTATO FRIES

12 medium-size sweet potatoes
4 cups vegetable oil

Peel the potatoes and cut them in half lengthwise. Place in a pot of boiling water and boil until they can be pierced with a fork, but with some resistance—about 25 minutes. Remove from the water. When cool, cut the potatoes into fingers.

In a deep fryer, heat the oil to 375 degrees. Drop in the potato fingers a few at a time (so that the temperature of the oil remains constant); fry until crisp and brown, about 3 minutes. Remove from the pan, drain on paper towels, and place in a warm oven while frying the next batch.

Note: Fry just before serving and do not reheat; the potatoes would become soggy.

DEEP-DISH PEACH PIE

PASTRY CRUST
1 cup all-purpose flour
1/2 teaspoon salt
1/4 pound cold butter
Cold water to dampen

Combine the flour and salt in a bowl and cut in the butter until the pieces are the size of peas. Add water tablespoon by tablespoon until the dough just holds together. Gather into a ball, wrap in plastic wrap, and let it rest for 30 minutes in the refrigerator.

FILLING
3 cups peeled, sliced ripe fresh peaches
1/4 cup all-purpose flour
1/2 cup light brown sugar
1/4 cup granulated sugar
1/2 teaspoon ground nutmeg
1/2 teaspoon ground ginger
1 teaspoon lemon juice
1/4 cup Amaretto
2 tablespoons unsalted butter

Combine all the ingredients, except the butter, and mix well. Transfer to a 10-inch pie pan and dot with the butter.

Preheat the oven to 375 degrees.

Roll out the dough until it is 1 1/2 inches larger than the circumference of the pie pan. Cover the pie pan with the dough, crimp the edges, and place the pie on a baking sheet (to catch any drips). Bake until browned, about 30 minutes. Serve lukewarm.

ASSORTED ANTIPASTO

FRITTATA WITH PROVENÇALE
TOMATO SAUCE

CHOCOLATE-DIPPED FRUIT
AND LADYFINGERS

(DINNER FOR SIX)

CHILLED WHITE AND RED
JUG WINES

MOVIE NIGHT

Sometimes, the food should support instead of star. Friends are coming by to see a miniseries or a great old movie on the VCR, and you want it to be more of an occasion than potato chips and sandwiches. Here's a menu both original and informal that is done before the audience arrives so you don't have to cook during the "good parts."

This is the night to use your flat-bottom bistro glasses. Serve the wines from carafes or those great pitchers you bought in Europe and never seem to use.

The frittata is large and a thing of beauty; it will keep people going to the end of *Gone with the Wind*. It comes to the buffet table in the skillet in which it was cooked. Only a guest with previous experience will know how to cope with it, so it should first be served by the cook at a break in the drama on screen. The "finger" dessert of chocolate-dipped sweets is rather choice; you might like to save it until the house lights come on again and break open a modest bottle of something bubbly.

ASSORTED ANTIPASTO

Assorted tinned fish (Italian tuna, anchovies,
    imported sardines)
Assorted salamis
Prosciutto and melon
Caponata
Olives
Pepperoncine
Artichoke hearts
Radishes
Cherry tomatoes
Celery strips
Green and red fresh pepper strips
Fresh fennel strips
Parmesan cheese, in small chunks
Imported Italian olive oil
Red wine vinegar
Thin bread sticks
Italian-style bread

These are only possibilities—your best Italian deli offers many more. The trick is to extract a balanced mini-menu from the excess of choices, playing the fresh and crunchy against the rich and salty. Arrange nicely on platters, with a pepper grinder and oil and vinegar cruets alongside. You will need plates, forks and lots of paper napkins. Guests help themselves.

FRITTATA WITH PROVENCALE TOMATO SAUCE

This is an Italian-grandmother frittata—thick, not thin, packed with cheese and sausage and vegetables, and slightly puffy.

18 eggs
1 tablespoon hot red pepper flakes
1 tablespoon fennel seeds
1 teaspoon Tabasco sauce
1/2 teaspoon dried oregano
4 tablespoons water
1/2 cup olive oil, in all
1 pound hot Italian sausages, cut into 1-inch slices
1/2 pound mushrooms, sliced thin
2 garlic cloves, sliced thin
2 large onions, coarsely chopped
2 green peppers, diced
2 sweet red peppers, diced
1 pound mozzarella, cut into 1-inch cubes
1/2 teaspoon salt
1 teaspoon freshly ground black pepper
1/2 pound mozzarella, sliced thin
4 cups (double recipe) Provençale Tomato Sauce
    (see Recipe Index)

Preheat the oven to 375 degrees.

Beat together the eggs, spices, and water in a bowl. Set aside.

Sauté the sausages, mushrooms, and garlic in 2 tablespoons of the oil until the sausage is no longer pink.

Drain off the oil and set the sausage mixture aside. In a large ovenproof skillet, sauté the onions in the remaining oil until just transparent. Add the sausage mixture, peppers, and cubes of mozzarella. Mix.

Pour in the eggs, season with salt and pepper, and, over medium-low heat, stir continuously from the bottom until the eggs begin to form curds. Place the skillet in the oven, uncovered, and bake until the eggs are set but still slightly loose, about 20 minutes. Remove from the oven and top in the center with a generous circle of mozzarella slices. Return to the oven until the cheese is puffy and brown, about 6 to 10 minutes.

Serve lukewarm, cut into wedges, with the tomato sauce alongside on each plate.

Note: Leftovers are fabulous. Have the frittata cold or reheat briefly in a microwave oven until the cheese melts again.

CHOCOLATE-DIPPED FRUIT AND LADYFINGERS

1 pound semisweet chocolate
1/4 cup vegetable oil
6 spears fresh pineapple
6 pieces candied ginger
6 dried apricots
6 large strawberries, with hulls
6 ladyfingers

Cut the chocolate into chunks and melt, with the oil, in the top of a double boiler over barely simmering water, stirring occasionally. When completely melted and very smooth and glossy, take off the heat and stir constantly until lukewarm.

Dip the fruits and ladyfingers halfway, one at a time, into the chocolate and put to dry on a baking sheet covered with wax paper. Refrigerate until needed. The fruits and ladyfingers should be dipped the day they are to be eaten.

Serve from one large platter, or, more conveniently, divide among three plates to be shared by two guests each.

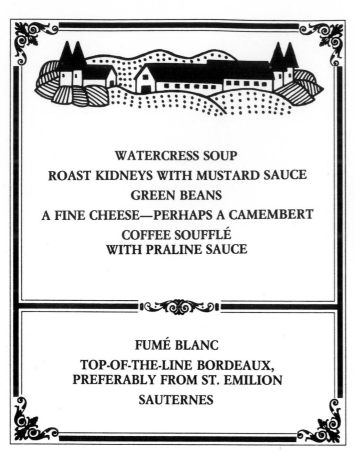

WATERCRESS SOUP
ROAST KIDNEYS WITH MUSTARD SAUCE
GREEN BEANS
A FINE CHEESE—PERHAPS A CAMEMBERT
COFFEE SOUFFLÉ
WITH PRALINE SAUCE

FUMÉ BLANC
TOP-OF-THE-LINE BORDEAUX, PREFERABLY FROM ST. EMILION
SAUTERNES

INTIMATE DINNER FOR TWO

WATERCRESS SOUP

3 tablespoons unsalted butter
2 leeks, white part only, halved and lengthwise and cross-cut at 1-inch intervals
4 large potatoes, peeled and cut in quarters
1 1/2 bunches watercress, roughly chopped
4 cups chicken broth
1/2 cup dry vermouth
4 or 5 black peppercorns
1 cup heavy cream
1/4 teaspoon freshly ground white pepper
1/8 teaspoon cayenne pepper
2 or 3 drops Tabasco sauce
1 teaspoon lemon juice

Intimate dinners are like intimate conversations—private, friendly, trusting and personal. The key to them is sharing and giving, whether it's a costly wine or something junky which you eat only in darkest secret.

What makes this dinner intimate? Why kidneys, of all things? Because your guest adores them and you know it. Why a soufflé? Because it's special and because your guest goes with you to the kitchen while you whip the egg whites.

From the lavishness of the soup to the cost of the wine, a meal like this is for a true friend.

The soup is hearty, country-elegant, and slightly peppery. It wants a well-chilled, fairly light wine with character. The kidney, with its darkly rich and slightly gamey flavor, needs a really full red wine, as fine a Bordeaux as you feel like springing for. This wine will also go perfectly with most full-flavored cheeses. For your soufflé, you can't do better than a Sauternes or a late harvest California Sauvignon. These come in half bottles, perfect for two.

For the sake of both ease and taste, the soup should be made ahead. Once refrigerated, it will keep for up to two days. The kidneys roast tranquilly in the oven during the first course; then the sauce is made in no more time than it takes the green beans to reheat. For a most attractive presentation, place the green beans in the center of the platter and surround them with the sliced kidneys.

While the soufflé bakes, finish up the red wine and serve a rich and hearty cheese, such as Vacherin or Époisse or a ripe Camembert.

In a heavy pot, melt the butter. Add the leeks, potato quarters, and half the watercress. Stir until the leeks soften. Add the chicken broth, vermouth, and peppercorns. Simmer. When the potatoes are done, in about 25 minutes, remove the equivalent of one potato, and set it aside.

Add the cream and remaining watercress and pureé the soup in a blender or food processor. Add the peppers, Tabasco sauce, and lemon juice. Taste and adjust the seasoning as desired. Return the reserved potato chunks to the soup.

ROAST WHOLE KIDNEYS WITH MUSTARD SAUCE

2 veal kidneys
Olive oil

Remove the fat from the core of the kidneys. The easiest method is to use a sharply pointed scissors. Rub the kidneys generously with the olive oil and place in a small baking pan.

Preheat the oven to 375 degrees. Roast the kidneys for 16 to 18 minutes for medium-rare. Remove the kidneys from the pan, cover them, and keep them warm. Pour off the excess fat and reserve the pan to make the sauce.

MUSTARD SAUCE
2 tablespoons meat glaze or *glace de viande*
(available commercially)
6 tablespoons water
2 teaspoons Dijon mustard, or to taste
2 tablespoons heavy cream
1 tablespoon brandy
1/4 teaspoon freshly ground black pepper

In the kidney roasting pan, simmer together the *glace de viande,* 4 tablespoons of the water, mustard, and cream. Stir constantly until well blended. Add the remaining water and the brandy and black pepper. Simmer for about 3 minutes. Strain into a sauceboat.

Cut the kidneys on a slant into slices 1/2 inch thick.
Note: Once sliced, the kidneys can be reheated beautifully in a microwave oven.

GREEN BEANS

1/2 pound French green beans *(haricots verts)*, with
ends trimmed
3 or 4 black peppercorns
2 tablespoons unsalted butter
Salt and freshly ground white pepper to taste

Blanch the green beans with the peppercorns in boiling water until tender but still crisp, 8 to 10 minutes. Immediately plunge them into cold water and then drain.

Melt the butter in a saucepan. Turn off the heat, add the green beans, and toss until they are coated. Cover and set aside. Reheat just before serving, seasoning with salt and pepper.

COFFEE SOUFFLE WITH PRALINE SAUCE

COFFEE INFUSION
1 to 4 tablespoons regular instant coffee
3 tablespoons instant espresso
3/4 cup boiling water

Make the infusion for flavoring this dessert to your own taste. For light, add to the espresso 1 to 2 tablespoons of coffee; for regular, 2 to 3 tablespoons; for dark, 3 to 4 tablespoons.

Put the coffees in a bowl and pour on the boiling water to dissolve. The mixture should be very thick. Set aside.

PRALINE SAUCE
1 1/2 cups milk
3 egg yolks
1/2 cup dark brown sugar
2 teaspoons coffee infusion
1 teaspoon vanilla extract
2/3 cup coarsely chopped pecans or walnuts

Scald the milk. In the top of a double boiler, off the heat, beat together the egg yolks, brown sugar, and the coffee infusion until a thick ribbon is formed when the beaters are lifted. Slowly stir in the hot milk. Cook and continue to stir over barely simmering water until you have a sauce with a light custard consistency.

Remove from the heat, stir in the vanilla, and adjust the flavor as desired with additional coffee infusion.

Stir in the chopped nuts. Cover and refrigerate. Reheat gently before serving with the soufflé.

SOUFFLÉ
3/4 cup milk
2 1/2 tablespoons unsalted butter (plus butter to
prepare the soufflé dish)
2 1/2 tablespoons flour
3 eggs, separated
3 tablespoons coffee infusion, or to taste
1/2 cup sugar

Butter a 3-cup soufflé dish. Preheat the oven to 425 degrees.

Scald the milk. Melt the butter in a second saucepan. Add the flour and stir for 1 minute. Pour in the milk and continue to stir until a thick base forms. Set aside to cool.

Stir the egg yolks and coffee infusion into the cooled sauce base.

Beat the egg whites, slowly adding the sugar, to form a soft-peaked meringue. Fold the whites into the sauce mixture. Pour into the soufflé dish and bake for 15 to 20 minutes for medium texture.

Notes: The entire coffee base can be prepared the day before. Cover the surface with plastic wrap and refrigerate. Set out at room temperature the next evening and just fold in the egg whites when ready to bake the soufflé.

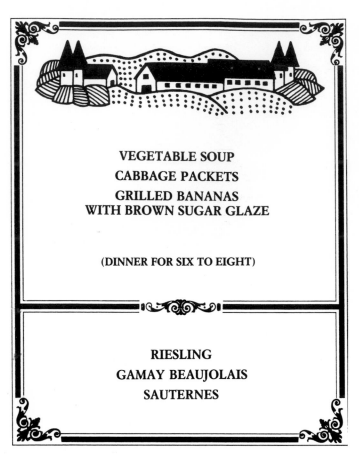

VEGETABLE SOUP
CABBAGE PACKETS
GRILLED BANANAS
WITH BROWN SUGAR GLAZE

(DINNER FOR SIX TO EIGHT)

RIESLING
GAMAY BEAUJOLAIS
SAUTERNES

CASUAL SUNDAY DINNER

When dark winter evenings come along, it's time for warmth and comfort. Since everything here but the dessert is done in advance, you, too, can have Sunday off. Sit around the kitchen table with close friends and offer them this simple, hearty meal.

No dry wines this time around. A Riesling (German or Californian), lightly sweet and faintly fruity, suits the soup. A Gamay Beaujolais will do the same trick with the cabbage. The bananas need a real honey-rich dessert wine.

Marketing is at the heart of this menu. It's loaded with vegetables, all available in fall and winter, and you have to be grateful for the produce markets we have today that provide all these growing things during the worst of weathers. To serve on Sunday, shop on Thursday or Friday.

VEGETABLE SOUP

4 large carrots, peeled
2 celery stalks
1/2 pound mushrooms
1 medium-size turnip, peeled
1 medium-size onion, peeled
1 bunch leeks, white part only, cut into chunks
2 medium-size boiling potatoes
1 bunch parsley
One 35-ounce can Italian plum tomatoes,
    with their juice
1 small zucchini
1 parsnip, peeled
1 small rutabaga, peeled
3 quarts chicken broth
3 tablespoons unsalted butter
2 tablespoons dried basil
2 tablespoons dried tarragon

1 teaspoon dried chervil
1 teaspoon dried rosemary
1 teaspoon dried oregano
1/2 teaspoon fennel seeds
8 black peppercorns
2 cups heavy cream
A little salt and a generous grinding of black pepper

Chop all the vegetables coarsely and put them in large pot with all the other ingredients, except the cream.

Simmer the soup until all the vegetables are soft, 30 to 45 minutes. Purée in batches, in a food processor or blender. Add the heavy cream. Check for seasoning, adding more salt and pepper to taste. This soup should be served very hot.

Note: The soup is better if it is made a day or two in advance. It also thickens while standing, so if it becomes too thick for your taste, add more chicken broth to thin it before serving.

CABBAGE PACKETS

16 large whole cabbage leaves
2 pounds ground pork
1 1/2 cups cooked rice
4 eggs, lightly beaten
2 onions, chopped fine
1 garlic clove, crushed
1 teaspoon dried dill
1 teaspoon salt
1/2 teaspoon freshly ground black pepper
2 tablespoons unsalted butter for the casserole
1/2 pound sliced bacon (see Note)
3 cups chicken broth
2 cups sour cream

Simmer the cabbage leaves in salted water for 4 minutes. Drain and cool.

Combine the pork, rice, eggs, onions, garlic, dill, salt, and pepper in a bowl. Divide the mixture evenly onto the cabbage leaves and roll into neat packages with the sides tucked in.

Place the rolls in a buttered flameproof casserole. Arrange the bacon slices on top. Add the chicken broth, cover, and bring to a boil. Let simmer with the cover askew for 1 hour. Cool completely and refrigerate. The rolls can be kept refrigerated for a day. Remove the surface fat and reheat to serve. Pass the sour cream at the table.

Note: It's not necessary but it is attractive if you remove the bacon before reheating and wrap each packet in a slice of freshly panfried bacon. Pour the pan juices into a serving casserole, arrange the packets in it, and then reheat in a slow oven, covered with aluminum foil or a lid.

GRILLED BANANAS WITH BROWN SUGAR GLAZE

3 to 4 bananas
3/4 cup rum
6 tablespoons heavy cream
1 cup dark brown sugar

Preheat the broiler.

Split the bananas lengthwise and cut them to fit into individual oven-to-table baking dishes. Combine the liquor and cream and divide the mixture equally among the dishes. Put in the bananas and sprinkle heavily with the sugar.

Place the dishes in the broiler with the broiling rack close to the flame. Cook until the sugar melts and glazes. Watch carefully; the sugar will burn if you turn your back on it! Expect the glazing to take 3 to 5 minutes. Remove and serve immediately.

Notes: Keep your measured ingredients separate until you are ready to make the dessert, and keep the liquor well covered so the alcohol won't evaporate. You just can't do this recipe ahead, except to have your ingredients at hand.

The liquor will catch fire. Don't worry, it will extinguish itself as soon as the alcohol has burned off, without doing any damage to your broiler or your dessert. This recipe also works beautifully for almost all fruits. If you choose a solid hard fruit, like apples or unripe pears, poach them lightly in sugar syrup first.

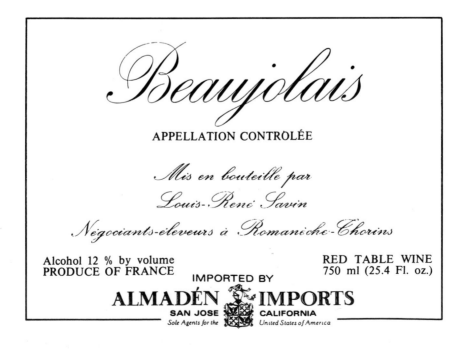

Beaujolais

APPELLATION CONTROLÉE

Mis en bouteille par
Louis-René Savin
Négociants-éleveurs à Romanèche-Thorins

Alcohol 12 % by volume
PRODUCE OF FRANCE

RED TABLE WINE
750 ml (25.4 Fl. oz.)

IMPORTED BY
ALMADÉN IMPORTS
SAN JOSE   CALIFORNIA
Sole Agents for the   *United States of America*

GIANT RAVIOLI
WARM SALAD OF QUAIL AND GARLIC CROUTONS
A FINE CHEESE
SYLLABUB

(LUNCH FOR FOUR)

GAVI OR VERNACCIA DI SAN GIMIGNANO
CHIANTI CLASSICO
SHERRY

WINTER LUNCH

Lunch in the new international European style, with an impressive modern version of pasta and birds presented on choice salad greens. You don't have to follow through with plates of such trendy design as those shown in the photographs—though it would be fun. The recipes in the menu are inwardly conservative, but their presentation is deliberately dramatic.

Your conversation-piece ravioli deserve a special wine such as Gavi, and the quail salad will show off Chianti Classico or another classy red to its best advantage, as will a good cheese. Use a delicious sherry to make the syllabub, and don't put the bottle away. Decant it and bring the decanter to the table with dessert.

As you are serving only four, this menu is designed to make it easy for you to show off a little and finish each course at the last minute if you want. However, if you have a microwave oven to reheat the cooked ravioli, they are a make-ahead dish. The dessert can be held for 3 hours or made in 5 minutes (basically, it is only whipped cream).

Put your attention to the quail salad. It's a matter of having everything lined up to go. Tackle it in the sequence in which the recipe is written: Set the bacon-covered quail in their roasting pan. Get the croutons ready for toasting. Make the dressing, to which you add a spoonful of drippings at the last. Arrange the lettuces on four plates. Preheat the broiler.

Then, when you are ready, the quail broil for about 4 minutes while the croutons toast briefly in the oven. Arrange the plates and take your time; the dish is not served piping hot.

GIANT RAVIOLI

1 medium-size onion, chopped
1 tablespoon unsalted butter
2 cups cooked chopped spinach
1 egg yolk
1 tablespoon grated Parmesan cheese
1 tablespoon heavy cream
1/2 teaspoon lemon juice
1/4 pound ham, cut into fine julienne
Ground nutmeg, freshly ground white pepper, and Tabasco sauce to taste
1 pound fresh pasta dough
2 cups Provençale Tomato Sauce (see Recipe Index)

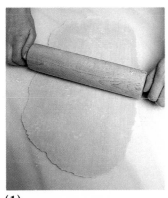
(1)

(2)

Sauté the onion in the butter in a small frying pan until it is transparent. In a food processor or blender, purée together the onion, spinach, egg yolk, Parmesan cheese, cream, and lemon juice. Then mix in the ham and season with nutmeg, pepper, and Tabasco sauce.

Roll pasta thin (1) into a rectangle approximately 12 by 24 inches. Cut into eight 6-inch squares (2). To assemble the ravioli, place equal amounts of the spinach mixture in the center of four of the pasta squares, leaving a 1/2-inch border. Moisten the edges with a pastry brush dipped in water (3). Top with the remaining squares and seal firmly (4–5). Trim the edges with a fluted pastry cutter if you wish (6). Poach the ravioli in a wide shallow pan of sim-

(3)

(4)

(5)

(6)

mering salted water until al dente, about 1 1/2 minutes. To drain, lift out with a slotted spoon one at a time. Reserve, covered, in a buttered glass baking dish and keep warm.

To serve, place one ravioli in the center of each guest's plate and add warmed Provençale tomato sauce either on or around it.

Note: The ravioli can be made and cooked a day ahead. Reheat them briefly in a microwave oven before serving.

WARM SALAD OF QUAIL AND GARLIC CROUTONS

QUAIL
8 quail, split in half
8 bacon strips, cut in half
1 tablespoon dried thyme

It's not hard to split the quail in half yourself with kitchen shears, but your butcher will certainly do it for you. Place them in a shallow pan, skin side up, and criss-

cross each half with pieces of bacon. Sprinkle with the thyme. Broil until the bacon is crisp, about 4 minutes. Reserve 1 tablespoon of drippings.

GARLIC CROUTONS
4 slices white bread
1 cup olive oil
3 garlic cloves, mashed

Remove the crusts from the bread and cut each slice into 4 triangles. Put the olive oil and garlic in a pan and gently simmer for 3 minutes. Dip the bread very lightly into the garlic oil. Discard the garlic and reserve the remaining oil. Place the bread on a baking sheet and toast on each side in the oven at 400 degrees.

DRESSING AND SALAD
1/2 to 3/4 cup garlic olive oil (above)
1 teaspoon balsamic vinegar
1 tablespoon red wine vinegar
1 tablespoon lemon juice
1 tablespoon pan drippings
Fresh greens (arugula, radicchio, lamb's lettuce, red-tip—two or three is enough)
Freshly ground black pepper

Combine the remaining garlic oil and vinegars, lemon juice, and pan drippings in a small bowl.

To serve, arrange on individual plates. Place the quail and the bacon on a bed of greens. Surround with the croutons and top generously with the dressing and black pepper.

SYLLABUB

Grated rind and juice of 1 lemon
Grated rind and juice of 1 lime
1/2 cup sugar
3 tablespoons sherry
2 tablespoons brandy
1/2 teaspoon vanilla extract
1 1/2 cups very cold heavy cream

Combine all the ingredients in a large bowl and beat until very thick. Spoon into individual stemmed glasses. Cover and chill.

Notes: Syllabub should be made no earlier than 3 hours before serving. If you have all the ingredients ready, it will take about 5 minutes from start to finish.

Heavy cream that is not ultra-pasteurized is best. If it is not available, use the cream labeled "whipping cream."

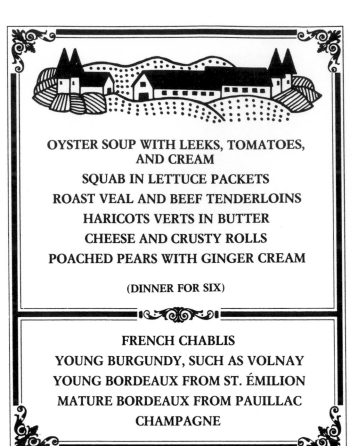

OYSTER SOUP WITH LEEKS, TOMATOES,
AND CREAM

SQUAB IN LETTUCE PACKETS

ROAST VEAL AND BEEF TENDERLOINS

HARICOTS VERTS IN BUTTER

CHEESE AND CRUSTY ROLLS

POACHED PEARS WITH GINGER CREAM

(DINNER FOR SIX)

FRENCH CHABLIS

YOUNG BURGUNDY, SUCH AS VOLNAY

YOUNG BORDEAUX FROM ST. ÉMILION

MATURE BORDEAUX FROM PAUILLAC

CHAMPAGNE

WINE BANQUET

Turn the clock back to another time, when life was gracious and luxurious, when people dressed for dinner, when an evening at a dinner was the equal of an evening at the opera. A five-course banquet, with a different wine for every course, is an experience to remember, whether you pull it off yourself or whether you are a guest. The extra courses, each in discreet amount, and the changing wines turn such dinners into occasions. There's work to do, but the effect is magical.

Changing wines with every course merely looks extravagant. The fact is, since there are six servings per bottle, all you need is one bottle of each. Almost any Burgundy or Bordeaux since 1981 can be considered young. The rich elegance of older Bordeaux will suit the French cheese, or the several cheeses, on your platter; consider having an Explorateur, l'Ami du Chambertin, and a chèvre. To start the evening, nothing pairs with oysters like Chablis. And nothing closes any dinner more festively than Champagne.

For this grand dinner of many courses and wines, though it is designed for only six people, you pace yourself as you would for a lesser meal served to a large number of guests: Either way, you spend time in the kitchen between courses and there is no need to rush things. The key to the timing of this menu is the one hour of roasting time and twenty minutes of resting for the tenderloins. All the other courses are prepared ahead almost to the point of serving. Someone other than the cook will, of course, take charge of the wines and the wine glasses. Thirty glasses are needed.

OYSTER SOUP

18 oysters, shucked, with their liquor
2 leeks, white part only, minced (see Note)
3 tablespoons unsalted butter
8 cups clam juice
2 cups canned plum tomatoes, with their juice
1 carrot, minced
1/2 cup minced fresh parsley
1/2 teaspoon freshly ground white pepper
1/2 teaspoon cayenne pepper
5 egg yolks, well beaten
2 cups heavy cream
2 scallions, minced

Note: Reserve the green part of the leeks for the *haricots verts*.

Drain the oysters and reserve their liquor. Sauté the leeks in the butter until soft.

In a large pot, combine the clam juice, reserved oyster liquor, leeks, tomatoes, carrot, parsley, and white and cayenne peppers. Bring to a boil and simmer for about 20 minutes. Strain. Poach the oysters in this broth until the edges curl—1 to 3 minutes. Remove the oysters and set them aside.

Combine the egg yolks and heavy cream in a bowl. Combine this mixture with the broth by first mixing hot broth, tablespoon by tablespoon, into the egg and cream mixture until it is of the same consistency as the broth. Then mix into the remaining broth. Cook until the soup thickens, stirring constantly. Do not boil.

To serve, garnish each bowl with 3 poached oysters and sprinkle with scallions.

Note: This soup can be made a day in advance. If so, refrigerate the cooked oysters separately, covering them with a bit of oyster liquor. When reheating, do not let the soup boil. Do not add the oysters until just before you are ready to serve.

SQUAB IN LETTUCE PACKETS

1 head iceberg lettuce
1 1/2 pounds mushrooms, minced
5 tablespoons unsalted butter, in all
2 tablespoons brandy
1 teaspoon dried chervil
1 teaspoon dried thyme
1/4 teaspoon ground ginger
4 drops Tabasco sauce
Salt and freshly ground black pepper to taste
3 whole squab breasts, boned and separated to make 6 pieces
6 mushrooms caps
1/4 cup dry vermouth
1/2 teaspoon lemon juice

Remove the core of the head of lettuce and remove the outside leaves **(1)**. Blanch 6 large perfect leaves in boiling water until flexible. Drain and set aside.

Sauté the minced mushrooms in 4 tablespoons of the butter until they are soft, adding the brandy, chervil, thyme, ginger, Tabasco sauce, and salt and pepper as they cook.

Preheat the oven to 400 degrees. Put the squab breasts in a pan and roast for 5 minutes for rare. Lay each breast in a lettuce leaf **(2)** with 1 heaping tablespoon of the mushroom mixture **(3)** and fold into a small, neat rectangular package **(4)**. Set aside, covered, in a dish that may be used in a microwave oven.

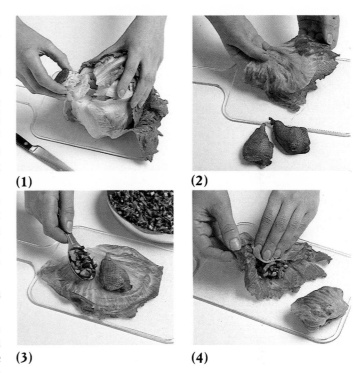

(1)   **(2)**

(3)   **(4)**

To serve, sauté the mushroom caps lightly in the remaining 1 tablespoon of butter in a small skillet. Remove from the pan and add the vermouth and a sprinkling of fresh lemon juice to the pan juices and reduce slightly. Reheat the squab packages briefly in the microwave, then place each package on a small plate and garnish with a mushroom cap and a spoonful of the pan juices.

Note: The squab packages can be made a day ahead, covered, and refrigerated. The mushroom caps should be sautéed just before serving. Reserve any extra mushroom stuffing; see Note at the end of the tenderloin recipe that follows.

VEAL AND BEEF TENDERLOINS

One 3-pound veal tenderloin, wrapped with barding fat and tied
One 3-pound piece beef tenderloin, wrapped with barding fat and tied

Bring the meats to room temperature. Preheat the oven to 425 degrees. Using a pan large enough to hold both roasts, first place the veal in the oven. After 15 minutes, put in the beef (which will cook faster than the veal). Roast the beef until it reaches an internal temperature of 120 degrees, and the veal until it reaches an internal temperature of 135 degrees. The entire cooking time should be about 1 hour. Transfer the tenderloins to a large platter and let both rest for 20 minutes before serving. Cut off the strings, remove the barding fat, and slice tenderloins thinly on the diagonal.

To serve, overlap the slices alternately, to best display the redness of the beef against the paleness of the veal, on a large platter garnished with the bundles of *haricots verts*.

Note: In order to roast and slice the tenderloins properly, they should each weigh at least 3 pounds. Therefore, you will have leftovers. They can be reheated in a microwave oven the next day and served with the extra mushroom stuffing from the squab recipe.

HARICOTS VERTS IN BUTTER

1 pound *haricots verts* (French green beans)
9 black peppercorns
Green part of 2 leeks
4 tablespoons unsalted butter
Salt and freshly ground black pepper to taste

Put the *haricots verts* and peppercorns in a pot of boiling water. Let cook until the beans are just done and still crisp, about 15 minutes. Immediately plunge into cold water. Remove and line up in rows. Working with 6 to 8 beans at a time, trim the ends evenly.

Boil the green part of leeks until soft. Lay flat on a towel to dry. Cut into thin strips and use to tie together each bunch of 6 to 8 beans.

Place the bundles in a dish that may be used in a microwave oven. Top each one with a small pat of butter and season with salt and pepper. Cover with plastic wrap.

To serve, reheat the beans in the microwave oven for 1 to 2 minutes, arrange them on the platter with the meat, and serve 2 bundles per person.

POACHED PEARS WITH GINGER CREAM

5 egg yolks, lightly beaten
1/2 cup sugar
1/4 teaspoon salt
3 cups milk
2 teaspoons vanilla extract
2/3 cup minced candied ginger
3 teaspoons unsalted butter at room temperature
6 whole Pears Poached in Red Wine (see Recipe Index)

In the top of a double boiler, combine the egg yolks, sugar, and salt. Scald the milk and stir it into the yolks very slowly, mixing all the time. Cook over barely simmering water, stirring constantly, until the mixture is thick enough to coat a spoon. Remove from the heat and add the vanilla extract. Add the ginger. When tepid, stir in the butter. Cover and refrigerate.

To serve, spoon the sauce into individual glass bowls and place a pear in each. Provide fruit knives and forks as well as dessert spoons.

CARPACCIO AND GREEN SAUCE
GRILLED RED SNAPPER WITH NIÇOISE SAUCE
ENDIVE WITH SWEET MUSTARD DRESSING
COFFEE ICE CREAM WITH LADYFINGERS

(DINNER FOR SIX)

GAMAY BEAUJOLAIS
WHITE RHÔNE
VIN SANTO

COUNTRY OR CITY SUMMER DINNER

Here's a happy ending to a summer day—and if you're in the city, set your table with a country look anyway. Each course is light and simple, chic but premeditated to be very easy to prepare. Grilling the fish al fresco makes for a cool, refreshing evening, but both an indoor and an outdoor method are given to cover all bases.

Serving beef before fish is a turn-about that allows you to serve red before white. With the carpaccio, California's Gamay Beaujolais is light, yet distinctive, a match for the well-seasoned green sauce. A white wine from France's Rhône Valley will have all the character necessary to match the grilled fish and its sauce. Try a Tuscan Vin Santo to complete the multinational wine menu.

CARPACCIO WITH GREEN SAUCE

GREEN SAUCE
2 cups Italian parsley leaves
3/4 cup olive oil
2 small cans flat anchovies, drained
One 3 1/2-ounce jar capers in vinegar, drained
3 garlic cloves
3 teaspoons Dijon mustard
2 teaspoons red wine vinegar
1 teaspoon lemon juice
Tabasco sauce to taste

Combine all the ingredients in a blender or food processor and process until smooth.

CARPACCIO
1 pound boneless shell steak, sliced thin
4 tablespoons olive oil

Have your butcher slice the beef as he would for scallopini. Pound the slices between sheets of oiled waxed paper until paper-thin. Place a few drops of oil on individual plates, arrange the slices of beef on the plates, and top with a few more drops of oil. Keep covered with plastic wrap until ready to serve. Top with a dollop of green sauce and pass the remainder of the sauce in a small bowl.

Note: Have the beef very cold when you pound it.

GRILLED RED SNAPPER WITH NICOISE SAUCE

NIÇOISE SAUCE
1 large onion, minced
1/4 cup olive oil
Two 35-ounce cans Italian plum tomatoes, coarsely
    chopped
1/2 cup small Provençal olives
2 tablespoons dry vermouth
2 large pieces orange peel, pith removed
1 teaspoon dried thyme
1 teaspoon dried rosemary
1 teaspoon dried oregano
1 teaspoon dried basil
Freshly ground black pepper to taste

Sauté the onion in the olive oil until it is transparent. Drain the tomatoes and combine with the onion. Add all the remaining ingredients and simmer for 15 minutes. Set aside and reheat to serve.

GRILLED RED SNAPPER I
Six 1/2-pound snapper fillets, with skin on
2 tablespoons olive oil

Rub each fillet with 1 teaspoon of oil and lay them on a broiling pan. Broil for 5 to 7 minutes with the pan on the lowest possible rung of the broiler. Do not turn. The top of the fillets should be barely flaky and the inside moist.

To serve, place one fillet on each plate and surround with Niçoise sauce.

Note: The cooked fillets can be reheated without drying out in a microwave oven.

GRILLED RED SNAPPER II
1/2 cup olive oil
1/2 cup white wine
2 tablespoons lemon juice
1 tablespoon balsamic vinegar
1 tablespoon sherry vinegar
1/4 cup chopped fresh basil leaves
1 teaspoon hot red pepper flakes
Three 2-pound red snappers, cleaned, with heads
    and tails on

Combine the liquids and seasonings in a pan large enough to hold the fish side by side. Slash the skins of the snappers, place them in the pan, and marinate, covered, in the refrigerator for 2 hours, turning after the first hour.

Oil the grill. When the coals are very hot, with an ashy glow, grill the snapper until the flesh is easily flaked, about 5 to 6 minutes per side. Baste every few minutes with the marinade. Transfer to a platter to fillet and serve.

Note: It is best to use fish grills that encase the fish on both sides, so they can be easily turned. One large two-sided hamburger grill also works, but be careful not to crush the fish when you latch the two sides together.

ENDIVE WITH SWEET MUSTARD DRESSING

2 tablespoons finely chopped shallots
2 tablespoons sweet German-style mustard, or to
    taste
3/4 cup olive oil
1 egg yolk
Generous sprinkling of freshly ground black pepper
3 heads endive

Combine the shallots and mustard. Little by little, whisk in the oil and then the egg yolk. Add the pepper.

On individual plates, arrange the endive leaves in a spoke pattern and spoon the dressing in the center.

Note: The dressing should be mustard-colored and smooth.

COFFEE ICE CREAM WITH LADYFINGERS

1 package ladyfingers
1/2 gallon of the very best coffee ice cream
Freeze-dried coffee granules

Toast the ladyfingers in the broiler until slightly crunchy. Scoop the ice cream into dessert bowls or stemmed glasses and sprinkle 1 teaspoon of coffee granules over each serving. Serve with the ladyfingers.

A not-too-sweet golden wine is just the thing here in summer, but espresso is good with this unashamedly labor-free dessert in winter.

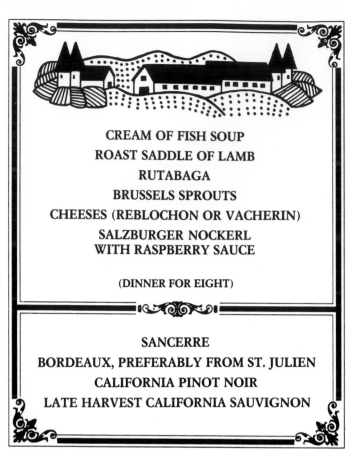

CREAM OF FISH SOUP

ROAST SADDLE OF LAMB

RUTABAGA

BRUSSELS SPROUTS

CHEESES (REBLOCHON OR VACHERIN)

SALZBURGER NOCKERL
WITH RASPBERRY SAUCE

(DINNER FOR EIGHT)

SANCERRE

BORDEAUX, PREFERABLY FROM ST. JULIEN

CALIFORNIA PINOT NOIR

LATE HARVEST CALIFORNIA SAUVIGNON

DINNER AT EIGHT

Hearty, warming winter dinners do not have to be heavy. The dessert here is light as air, the vegetables are steamed, the meat is simply roasted, and the soup—well, what's a little cream?

Try a lively flavorful Sancerre with the soup. A Bordeaux—it need not be an old one—always fits with lamb, while a hearty Pinot Noir will follow nicely. And the foamy delicacy of the dessert will flatter your honied sweet wine.

Pick one person to be in charge of pouring the wine; too many helping hands cause confusion. You need thirty-two wine glasses, which by no means need to be of matching style—four different sets of eight each will do it. A wine "sideboard" set up in advance is recommended. Removing glasses used for the earlier courses makes sense so long as it is not done abruptly.

As in any menu with a roast, your timing is guided by the roasting time—here up to an hour and a quarter, including resting time, for the lamb. Guests should be seated at the table for the soup about 15 minutes before the lamb is ready to be carved. What counts, though, is not split-second serving; it's the right internal temperature and resting for the meat.

See the **Recipe Index** for the Brussels sprouts, which are cooked ahead and reheated in butter, as are the rutabagas.

Four courses with four wines is an entire evening's entertainment. Prepare ahead, but don't rush. The cook, too, is meant to enjoy it.

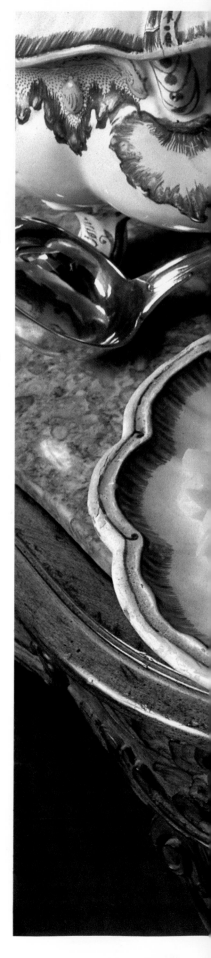

CREAM OF FISH SOUP

THE BASE
8 cups clam juice
2 cups white wine
3 pounds fish heads and trimmings (see Note)
1 bunch fresh parsley
1 small onion, chopped coarsely
2 celery stalks, chopped coarsely
12 black peppercorns
2 bay leaves
8 large shrimp, in their shells
One 1 1/4-pound live lobster

Bring the clam juice to a boil in a large pot. Add all the ingredients, except the shrimp and lobster. Continue to boil for 10 minutes. Reduce the heat to a low simmer, add the shrimp and poach for 2 minutes. Remove the shrimp; drain and shell them over a bowl. Reserve the meat. Return the shells and juices to the pot.

Poach the lobster in the broth for 8 minutes. Remove the lobster and shell it. Reserve the meat and return shells and juices to the pot. Continue to cook for 30 minutes at a low simmer. Pass the soup through a fine sieve into a bowl, pressing hard on the solids. Let cool completely, uncovered, and refrigerate, uncovered or only loosely covered, until needed.

Note: Fishmongers are happy to give you fish heads and trimmings. Rinse them well. Avoid trimmings of strong-tasting fish like salmon or mackerel; ask for whitefish and flatfish.

FINISHING
6 egg yolks, lightly beaten
4 cups heavy cream
1/4 teaspoon cayenne pepper
1 teaspoon lemon juice

Bring the soup base to a boil. Mix the egg yolks and cream together. Add soup to this mixture, tablespoon by tablespoon, until it is of the same consistency as the soup. Then mix this back into the soup and season with the cayenne and lemon juice. Cut the shrimp and lobster meat into large pieces (they should be at room temperature) and drop them into the hot soup just before serving.

Serve from a tureen or an attractive cooking pot.

Note: If you reheat the soup, do not let it boil as it will curdle.

ROAST SADDLE OF LAMB

One whole saddle of lamb
1 cup olive oil
4 tablespoons dried rosemary

Place the lamb in a baking pan, fat side up. Combine the oil and rosemary and pat onto the lamb. Marinate at room temperature for at least 2 hours.

Preheat the oven to 400 degrees. Roast the lamb until it reaches an internal temperature of 135 degrees, 45 to 60 minutes. Let the lamb rest for 15 minutes before carving.

To serve, carve at the table: cut the saddle into long thin lateral slices, with the grain, one side at a time.

Note: Have your butcher cut off the two bottom flanks of the saddle and save them for a lunch or family dinner. They are terrific broiled but will interfere with the roasting time of the saddle.

RUTABAGA

2 large rutabagas, peeled
6 black peppercorns
4 tablespoons unsalted butter
Salt to taste

Cut the rutabagas into slices about 3/8 inch thick, then cut the slices into sticks, as for slim French-fried potatoes. Cook with the peppercorns in boiling water until tender but still crisp, about 10 minutes. Immediately plunge into cold water. Drain.

Melt the butter in a saucepan. Turn off the heat. Add the rutabagas and toss until coated. Reheat to serve, seasoning with salt to taste.

SALZBURGER NOCKERL WITH RASPBERRY SAUCE

2 tablespoons unsalted butter
8 eggs, separated
2 teaspoons vanilla extract
2 tablespoons flour
4 tablespoons granulated sugar
Confectioner's sugar
Double recipe Raspberry Sauce (see Recipe Index), warm

Preheat the oven to 375 degrees. Place the butter in an oval or oblong 8-by-10-by-2-inch baking dish and bring to a sizzle in the oven.

Whisk together the egg yolks, vanilla, and flour. Whip the whites, adding the sugar gradually. When stiff, fold the whites carefully into the egg-yolk mixture. Using a spatula, place large mounds of the batter in the hot baking dish. Do not smooth; the look should be uneven.

Return the dish to the oven and bake for 10 minutes. Remove from the oven and sift confectioner's sugar over the top. To serve, spoon the warmed sauce onto individual plates and top with a mound of the Nockerl.

Notes: If you have all your ingredients ready beforehand, this dessert will take 15 minutes. Prepare it during the cheese course.

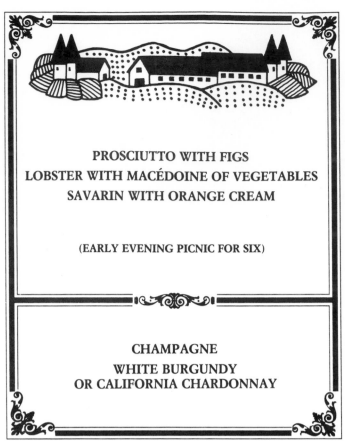

PROSCIUTTO WITH FIGS
LOBSTER WITH MACÉDOINE OF VEGETABLES
SAVARIN WITH ORANGE CREAM

(EARLY EVENING PICNIC FOR SIX)

CHAMPAGNE
WHITE BURGUNDY
OR CALIFORNIA CHARDONNAY

ELEGANT PICNIC

In spirit, this is a grown-up picnic designed for a special occasion. It doesn't require a Rolls Royce for transport nor crystal and silver, though the menu will live up to as much luxury in the presentation as you want to give it.

Begin with Champagne, perhaps a blanc de blancs from California. To follow, Chardonnay accompanies lobster as well as picture hats go with garden-party dresses. Polish off the remaining Champagne with your savarin.

This elegant meal requires some inelegant props, chiefly an extra-large Styrofoam cooler and a large utilitarian aluminum pan at least 2 inches deep to serve as platter for the lobster. By the middle of the day, every-thing will have been made ahead and stored in the refrigerator. When it's time to leave, put sealed bags of ice in the cooler (it will serve later to cool the wine). Pack all the food in the cooler, with the lobster on top. If you then have a nice looking straw trunk in which to put the cooler and to serve as "sideboard" at the picnic, so much the better. The wine travels in its own carrier and the savarin in a covered cake tin or a basket.

Gilded stemmed plastic wine glasses make quite an effect. Any silverware, including the best, will do, and you need a couple of sharp knives, attractive plastic plates, and plenty of real napkins. Don't forget the pepper mill.

PROSCIUTTO WITH FIGS

1 1/2 pounds prosciutto, sliced thin
12 ripe figs
Freshly ground black pepper

Arrange prosciutto on a platter and cover with plastic wrap. Store the figs in a plastic container. Refrigerate both.

To serve, "flower-cut" the figs into sixths, arrange on the platter, and grind pepper over all.

LOBSTER WITH MACEDOINE OF VEGETABLES

MACÉDOINE
1/2 pound fresh green beans, cut into 1/2-inch pieces
1/2 pound carrots, diced
Two 10-ounce packages frozen peas
1 cup mayonnaise (see Note)
Salt and freshly ground black pepper to taste

Poach the vegetables separately in simmering water until tender but still crisp, about 5 minutes for each. Drain well. While the vegetables are still warm, combine them with the mayonnaise and season with salt and pepper.

LOBSTER
Six 1- to 1 1/2-pound lobsters
1/2 cup mayonnaise
1/4 cup finely cut chives
Lettuce leaves

Poach or steam the lobsters until shells are red, about 10 minutes. Let cool. Split the heads of the lobsters on the underside and remove the small and large claws. With kitchen shears, cut away the underside of the tail shells and remove the tail meat in one piece. Remove the tomalley and coral from the body and reserve them. Keep the head and tail shells attached; score the shells lengthwise from head to tail on the inside so the two sides can be gently pried open. Clean the shells and dry them.

Fill the lobster shells with the macédoine of vegetables. Devein the tail meat, slice it, and arrange it on top of the vegetables. Place the filled shells close together in a large shallow pan, using fresh lettuce leaves to fill the spaces and steady the lobsters. Cover with plastic wrap and refrigerate.

Shell the large claws and combine the claw meat, tomalley, and coral with the mayonnaise. Store in a screwtop jar in the refrigerator. Chop the chives and put them in a small container with a cover.

To serve, place one lobster on each plate and mound equal portions of the claw meat and dressing alongside. Top with the chives.

Note: The mayonnaise used for Crab Meat Salad on page 111 is also good for this lobster dish.

SAVARIN WITH ORANGE CREAM

SAVARIN
1 package active dry yeast
1 1/4 cups water, in all
1 1/2 cups sifted all-purpose flour
1 tablespoon sugar
1/2 teaspoon salt
3 eggs
1/4 cup milk
1/4 pound plus 2 tablespoons unsalted butter, softened
1 tablespoon grated orange rind
1/2 teaspoon orange extract
1 cup dark rum
1/2 cup orange liqueur

Combine the yeast and 1/4 cup of the water and stir well.

Combine the flour, sugar, and salt. Stir in the yeast, eggs, and milk and beat well. Add the butter, orange rind, and orange extract and beat well. Pour the batter into a 9-inch ring mold, filling it half full. Cover with a towel and let rise for 1 hour. Bake at 400 degrees until brown, about 30 minutes. When the savarin is done, unmold it onto a wire rack over a platter.

Warm together the remaining 1 cup of water and the rum and liqueur. Using a baster, gradually saturate the savarin with the rum mixture. Reserve 1 tablespoon for the orange cream.

ORANGE CREAM
6 egg yolks
1/4 cup sugar
1 tablespoon rum mixture (above)
1/4 cup orange juice
2 cups whipping cream

1 pint blueberries

Beat together the egg yolks and sugar until very thick and almost white. Stir in the rum mixture and orange juice. Whip the cream and fold it into the yolk mixture. Store in a screwtop jar and refrigerate.

Place the savarin on a plate in a large cake tin, spoon the blueberries into the center, and cover with the lid.

Serve the blueberries and slices of savarin on individual plates with orange cream spooned over them.

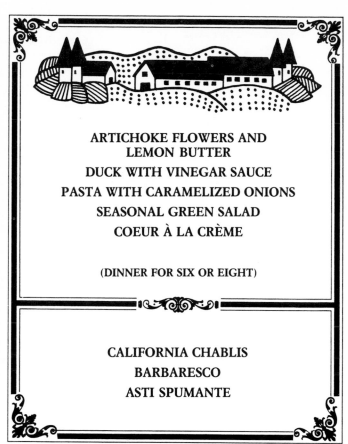

ARTICHOKE FLOWERS AND
LEMON BUTTER
DUCK WITH VINEGAR SAUCE
PASTA WITH CARAMELIZED ONIONS
SEASONAL GREEN SALAD
COEUR À LA CRÈME

(DINNER FOR SIX OR EIGHT)

CALIFORNIA CHABLIS
BARBARESCO
ASTI SPUMANTE

INFORMAL DINNER

ARTICHOKE FLOWERS AND LEMON BUTTER

6 medium-size artichokes
1 tablespoon olive oil
12 tablespoons unsalted butter
2 tablespoons lemon juice, or to taste
Salt and cayenne pepper to taste

Trim the base and leaf tips of the artichokes. Boil or steam them until tender, 35 to 40 minutes. Let them cool and drain upside down on a rack.

Artichokes invite becoming presentations. Here are two options: For artichoke flowers, remove all the leaves and the chokes. (Sprinkle a few drops of olive oil on the heart to prevent discoloring.) Arrange the leaves around the heart in the design of a flower. Serve at room temperature.

Or, quicker, and can be done well ahead: Gently spread apart the leaves of the artichokes and take out the papery center leaves. Reserve the last layer of thin leaves just over the choke; it should come out in one piece in the shape of a small coolie hat. Scoop out all the choke. Just before serving, pour a little of the lemon butter into the hollow of each artichoke and use the "hats" as lids.

At serving time, melt the butter and add the lemon juice and salt and cayenne pepper. Pour into a sauceboat and pass at the table. For 8 artichokes, add another 1/2 stick of butter and adjust the seasoning.

It is a winter Sunday and you're dining in a French country house. Outside the windows, sheep are grazing in the sun while chamber music whispers in your ears. Your menu is presented . . .

Style, complexity of taste, and ease of preparation are the virtues of this meal. You can sit and talk, relax with an apéritif, and when your guests are ready, you can seem to toss this one off.

With the artichokes, almost any light, not very tart white will do the trick. The duck is something else again. Its flavor is smooth, rich, and complicated and wants a big, flavorful red. After a fresh salad without wine, have a sparkling wine with dessert—Asti Spumante or anything attractive, so long as it has bubbles.

The only last-minute steps in this meal should be warming the lemon butter, cooking and dressing the pasta, and tossing the salad. The duck *has* to be done ahead to achieve its full flavor; the recipe allows for second helpings.

DUCK WITH VINEGAR SAUCE

Legs and thighs from 6 young ducks (see Note)
3 tablespoons duck fat or unsalted butter
1 to 1 1/2 whole heads garlic, broken apart, cloves
    unpeeled
1 cup best quality red wine vinegar
1 tablespoon dried tarragon or 2 tablespoons
    chopped fresh tarragon leaves
1 cup Provençale Tomato Sauce (see Recipe Index)
8 to 10 sprigs Italian parsley
1 1/2 cups chicken broth
1 teaspoon meat glaze or *glace de viande* (available
    commercially)
1 cup red wine
1/2 pound mushrooms, stems removed and caps
    sliced thin
4 tablespoons unsalted butter
1/4 cup dry vermouth
Freshly ground black pepper

Melt the duck fat in a heavy pan. Brown the duck pieces with the unpeeled garlic cloves over medium heat. (Be careful; they will stick and splatter). When browned, remove the duck pieces and garlic and set aside separately.

Pour off the fat from the pan. Add the vinegar and deglaze the pan. Add the tarragon, tomato sauce, parsley, chicken broth, meat extract, red wine, and the reserved garlic cloves. Simmer, stirring occasionally, for 15 minutes.

Separately, sauté the sliced mushrooms in the butter, adding the dry vermouth and pepper to taste. Set aside.

Place the duck pieces in a casserole. Strain the sauce over them, pushing hard on the solids. Add the mushrooms and their juices to the casserole. Refrigerate.

To serve, first remove the hardened fat. Reheat the casserole for 15 to 20 minutes. Taste and adjust the seasoning as desired with vinegar, salt, pepper, and tarragon.

Notes: Have the butcher cut up the ducks, keeping each leg and thigh in one piece. The legs should be "frenched": Cut off the tip and push the flesh up the bone to make a lollipop form. Since ducks are usually sold whole, reserve the breasts; they freeze beautifully. There is a duck-breast recipe on page 113.

PASTA WITH CARAMELIZED ONIONS

The onions are prepared ahead. Have a large pot of water simmering during the first course. Between courses reheat the onions and cook the pasta.

3 pint baskets pearl onions
8 tablespoons unsalted butter
2 tablespoons dark brown sugar
Salt and freshly ground black pepper to taste
1 1/2 pounds flat pasta, such as fettuccine

Blanch the onions in boiling water for 15 to 30 seconds. Drain, squeeze off their skins, and cut off the root ends. Sauté the onions in the butter until they are caramelized, 15 to 20 minutes. As they cook, season the onions with the sugar and salt and pepper.

Cook the pasta until al dente. Drain; and then toss with the onions.

To serve, arrange the pasta on plates in nests. Place 1 or 2 duck pieces in the center and spoon the sauce and mushrooms over the duck only.

Note: Pearl onions are particularly attractive, but take a while to skin. This dish can be made with regular onions. Use 3 large Bermuda onions, cut into large chunks. Sauté in butter until caramelized and continue as for the pearl onions.

COEUR A LA CREME

It takes European savoir-faire to make something so pretty from cottage cheese. The full effect requires porcelain *coeur à la crème* molds. In a pinch, you can make this is a colander, but you won't get the heart-shaped charm.

1 1/2 pounds cream-style cottage cheese
3 tablespoons confectioner's sugar
3 teaspoons vanilla extract
1 1/2 cups whipping cream
Whites of 4 eggs
Extra confectioner's sugar for topping
2 cups Raspberry or Strawberry Sauce (see Recipe
    Index)
1 1/2 cups raspberries or sliced strawberries

Push the cottage cheese through a sieve into a bowl. Stir in the confectioner's sugar and vanilla extract.

Beat the cream until soft peaks form. Fold into the cottage cheese mixture. Beat the egg whites until stiff. Fold into the mixture. Taste and adjust the seasoning with more sugar and vanilla to taste.

Line each mold with damp cheesecloth, leaving a generous overhang. Spoon in enough cheese mixture to nearly fill the molds and fold the extra cloth over the tops. Place the molds on a wire rack in a shallow pan. Cover each with a small saucer weighted with a can of tuna or some other even weight. Refrigerate overnight.

Liquid will have formed. Wipe off the bottoms of the molds. Cut away the cheesecloth from the tops. Invert each mold carefully onto a dessert plate and remove the remaining cheesecloth. (Should a heart get broken, simply pat it back together.)

Sprinkle with confectioner's sugar and serve with the sauce and berries.

Note: Coeur à la Crème must be prepared at least 24 hours in advance; it can be unmolded before the guests arrive.

FRESH-SQUEEZED MIXED-UP JUICE
WAFFLES WITH STRAWBERRY BUTTER
BAKED THICK-SLICED BACON
VANILLA CUSTARD
COFFEE

(BREAKFAST FOR FOUR)

CHAMPAGNE

SUNDAY BREAKFAST

The objective here is get-up-late luxury—it's breakfast, but it serves as brunch/lunch. Make the strawberry butter and the vanilla custard on Saturday. The rest of the meal is comfortable breakfast cooking, with guests in the kitchen.

Most people are creatures of habit at breakfast, even on Sunday. It's not a time for innovations. So the changes here—a refreshing mix of fruit juices, something new to go with waffles, bacon done a fail-safe way—are small but will not go unappreciated.

This is not the time for vintage bottlings or costly imports. What you're looking for is sparkle to mix with the fruit juices and pleasant sipping thereafter. Depending on the hour, extra champagne may not be out of line.

FRESH-SQUEEZED MIXED-UP JUICE

Juice of 2 large grapefruits
Juice of 6 juice oranges
Juice of 1 lime
2 cups cranberry juice
Sugar to taste
Champagne

Combine the four juices in a pitcher. Taste for sweetness and add sugar if necessary.

To serve, fill large goblets halfway with juice, add ice, and top with chilled champagne. Stir to blend.

WAFFLES WITH STRAWBERRY BUTTER

STRAWBERRY BUTTER
1 pound unsalted butter at room temperature
One 10-ounce package frozen strawberries, thawed
** and drained**
2 tablespoons confectioner's sugar

In a food processor, whip together the butter, strawberries, and sugar until light and fluffy. Serve in a crock to accompany the waffles—or in a silver bowl, depending on the style you have in mind for this Sunday morning.

Note: This can be made the day before. If the mixture starts to separate, just rewhip before serving. This butter is also wonderful on hot biscuits.

WAFFLES
1 3/4 cups all-purpose flour
2 teaspoons baking powder
1/2 teaspoon salt
2 tablespoons sugar
3 eggs, separated
1 3/4 cups milk
6 tablespoons butter, melted

Into a bowl, sift the flour together with the baking powder, salt, and sugar. In a separate bowl, beat the egg yolks lightly; then mix in the milk and butter. Combine this with the flour mixture.

In another bowl, beat the egg whites until they form firm peaks; then fold them into the batter. Use a preheated waffle iron and bake until the steam has stopped coming from around the edge of the iron, usually about 5 minutes.

BAKED THICK-SLICED BACON

1 pound thick-sliced lean smoked bacon

Preheat the oven to 450 degrees. Put the bacon slices on a rack in a baking pan and bake, without turning, for 20 to 30 minutes, or until browned. Drain on paper towels and serve while still warm.

VANILLA CUSTARD

2 cups half-and-half
1/4 cup sugar
1/8 teaspoon salt
5 egg yolks
2 teaspoons vanilla extract

Scald the half-and-half. Stir in the sugar and salt and remove from the heat. Let cool slightly. Preheat the oven to 350 degrees.

In a bowl, beat the egg yolks. Gradually add the warm milk, stirring constantly. Continue to stir (do not beat) and add the vanilla. Pour into 4 large custard cups. Place the cups in a shallow baking pan and pour water into the pan to one-half the depth of the cups. Cover with a baking sheet or aluminum foil. Bake and test after 25 minutes; the custards are done when a small pointed knife inserted off-center into the custard comes out clean. Remove the cups from the hot water. Let cool, uncovered, on a wire rack; then cover and refrigerate.

Note: These may be made a day ahead.

CHICKEN-MUSHROOM SOUP
BRAISED LAMB SHANKS
FLAGEOLETS WITH ONION AND TOMATO
MIXED GREEN SALAD
BAKED APRICOT WHIP WITH ICE CREAM

(DINNER FOR EIGHT)

WHITE ZINFANDEL
RED RHÔNE,
SUCH AS CHÂTEAUNEUF-DU-PAPE
LATE HARVEST SAUVIGNON BLANC

INFORMAL JANUARY DINNER

Impressive dinners can be made from simple, inexpensive foods. Start with a delightful, warming chicken soup. Follow with a classic bistro combination, lamb and flageolets, the dried beans so popular in France. The apricot whip is pure, old-fashioned American, but it works.

This menu is both hearty and elegant, an invitation to present wines with the same characteristics. First, the "blush" version of Califor-nia's popular Zinfandel; then Châteauneuf-du-Pape, one of the few great wines produced in the south of France. It is a country gentleman, well-bred but forthright. This pairs as well with the flavorful lamb and beans as red Bordeaux does with an aristocratic saddle of lamb. Apricots have been called the perfect fruit to complement wine; therefore, your choice of a dessert wine can be fairly delicate and subtly sweet. If you can't find a late harvest Sauvignon, a German Auslese is an appropriate alternative.

CHICKEN MUSHROOM SOUP

2 quarts chicken broth
1 small chicken, cut into eight pieces, and giblets
1 pound mushrooms, stems separated and caps sliced thin
1 bunch parsley sprigs
1 small onion, peeled
6 black peppercorns
1 tablespoon unsalted butter
1/4 cup dry sherry

Pour the chicken broth into a large pot and add the chicken, the giblets (discarding the livers), mushroom stems, parsley, onion, and peppercorns. Partially cover the pot and simmer until the chicken begins to come off the bones, about 40 minutes.

Remove the chicken. Cut the breast meat into julienne strips and reserve. (Save the rest of the chicken meat for a salad.) Strain the soup, pressing down hard on the solids, and return the liquid to the pot.

Simmer the sliced mushroom caps in the butter and sherry. Add the reserved chicken and the mushrooms and their pan juices to the pot. Taste for seasoning.

Note: Boiling the livers in the stock can make it bitter.

BRAISED LAMB SHANKS

Eight 1 1/4-pound lamb shanks, outside fat trimmed
6 tablespoons olive oil
3/4 cup red wine
3/4 cup beef or chicken broth
6 garlic cloves, peeled
1 teaspoon dried tarragon
1 teaspoon dried basil
1 teaspoon dried rosemary
1/2 teaspoon dried thyme
8 to 10 parsley sprigs
6 black peppercorns

In a heavy skillet, brown the lamb shanks on all sides in the oil. Remove the lamb and pour off the oil. Add the remaining ingredients and bring the liquid to a boil, scraping the bottom of the pan with a wooden spoon. Return the lamb shanks and cook, covered, over low heat, turning occasionally, for about 1 1/4 hours, or until the meat is tender.

When done, transfer the lamb to a deep serving platter and keep warm. Strain the cooking liquid into a saucepan. Reduce over high heat until syrupy, 12 to 15 minutes. Pour over the lamb shanks.

FLAGEOLETS WITH ONION AND TOMATOES

2 cups dried flageolets, soaked in water overnight
4 cups chicken broth
1 cup dry white wine
1 medium-size onion, cut into chunks
2 teaspoons salt
One 35-ounce can plum tomatoes, drained
2 bay leaves
1/2 tablespoon dried tarragon
1/2 tablespoon dried basil
1 tablespoon chopped fresh parsley
Coarsely ground black pepper to taste

Drain the beans and put them in a large pot along with the chicken broth, white wine, and 3 cups of water. Bring to a boil, reduce the heat, and add the remaining ingredients, except the pepper. Simmer, partially covered, until the beans are soft and the juices absorbed, about 2 to 2 1/2 hours.

Serve from the cooking pot after adding a generous grinding of pepper.

BAKED APRICOT WHIP WITH ICE CREAM

2 cups dried apricots
1 cup sweet white dessert wine
1 large strip lemon peel
5 egg whites
1/2 teaspoon cream of tartar
2 teaspoons grated lemon rind
1 quart rich vanilla ice cream

Combine the apricots, wine, and lemon peel in a saucepan and cook, partially covered, until the apricots are mushy, about 30 minutes. Purée in a blender or processor. Fold in the grated lemon rind and set aside until cool.

Preheat the oven to 350 degrees. Whip together the egg whites and cream of tartar until stiff. Fold in the apricot purée. Pour the mixture into a buttered and sugared 9-inch soufflé dish. Put the dish in a roasting pan and pour in hot water to come halfway up the sides of the dish. Bake until firm, about 1 hour.

Spoon into dessert dishes and add a scoop of slightly softened ice cream to each portion.

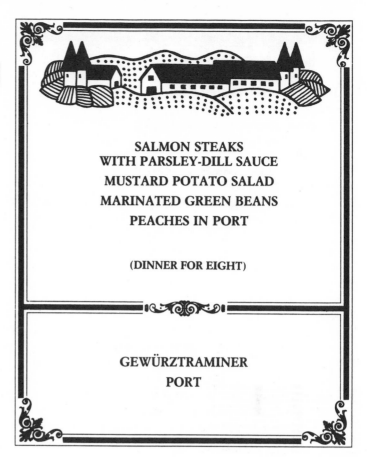

SALMON STEAKS
WITH PARSLEY-DILL SAUCE
MUSTARD POTATO SALAD
MARINATED GREEN BEANS
PEACHES IN PORT

(DINNER FOR EIGHT)

GEWÜRZTRAMINER
PORT

MIDSUMMER DINNER

A warm evening calls for cool elegance in the menu. This do-ahead dinner fills the bill perfectly. The salmon, which is poached in a spicy white wine, is fresh, both in look and flavor. And after a bath in Port, the peaches are both a sweet and refreshing way to top off the meal.

How important wine is in the kitchen is illustrated in this menu. It's a showcase in which you use wine to prepare the salmon and the peaches and then are rewarded by the distinctive, quite out of the ordinary flavors of the finished dishes. Use the same wine in the kitchen as you will serve with each course. Don't, however, reach for a vintage Port. A ruby Port or the equivalent from Portugal or California is perfectly appropriate here.

SALMON STEAKS WITH PARSLEY-DILL SAUCE

1 bottle Gewürztraminer
3 cups water
1 celery stalk, chopped
2 carrots, chopped
1 medium-size onion, chopped
10 parsley sprigs
4 dill sprigs
12 black peppercorns, crushed
1 teaspoon salt
8 medium-size salmon steaks, cut 1 inch thick, at
    room temperature

Combine all the ingredients, except the salmon steaks, to make a *court-bouillon*. Bring the mixture to a boil, cover loosely, and simmer for 20 minutes. Strain over the salmon steaks in two skillets (see Note). Bring to a boil again, cover, and reduce the heat. Cook on top of the stove for 8 to 10 minutes. Remove from the heat, let cool in the poaching broth, and then transfer, still in the broth, to the refrigerator. Drain 30 minutes before serv-ingtime and let the salmon come to room temperature.

Note: You can also place the 8 steaks in a baking pan. When you have brought the broth back to a boil on top of the stove, transfer the pan to a preheated 375-degree oven and cook the fish for 8 to 10 minutes.

PARSLEY-DILL SAUCE
1 1/2 cups mayonnaise
1 tablespoon lemon juice
3 tablespoons chopped fresh dill
1 1/2 tablespoons chopped fresh parsley
3/4 teaspoon freshly ground pepper, preferably
    white

In a mixing bowl, combine all the ingredients and mix well. Pass in a sauceboat at the table. Cover and chill in the refrigerator until ready to serve.

MUSTARD POTATO SALAD

6 tablespoons olive oil
6 tablespoons wine vinegar
1 1/2 tablespoons Dijon mustard
2 tablespoons chopped fresh parsley
Salt and freshly ground white pepper to taste
24 small new potatoes, peeled (about 3 pounds)

Combine the oil, vinegar, mustard, parsley, and season--ings in a bowl. Blend well and set aside.

Steam or boil the potatoes until soft but still firm. Im-mediately cut them into slices or chunks and toss with the mustard sauce. Let cool at room temperature and then refrigerate after tasting for seasoning. Serve cool but not chilled.

MARINATED GREEN BEANS

2 pounds green beans, ends trimmed
1/4 cup olive oil
2 tablespoons wine vinegar
Salt and freshly ground white pepper to taste

Boil the beans in salted water until crisp-tender. Drain. While still warm, toss the beans with the oil, vinegar, and salt and pepper. Refrigerate. Serve cool but not chilled.

PEACHES IN PORT

1/2 cup Port
1 tablespoon lemon juice
2 tablespoons sugar
8 ripe peaches
1 cup whipping cream
2 tablespoons confectioner's sugar

In a glass bowl stir together the Port, lemon juice, and sugar.

Dip each peach briefly in boiling water; then remove the skin. Cut the peaches in slices into the bowl. Stir well, cover, and refrigerate for 2 to 6 hours. Remove the peaches from the refrigerator at least half an hour before serving.

Just before serving, whip the cream together with the confectioner's sugar and fold in 2 tablespoons of the Port syrup. Spoon the peaches and a little syrup into dessert bowls and top with dollops of whipped cream.

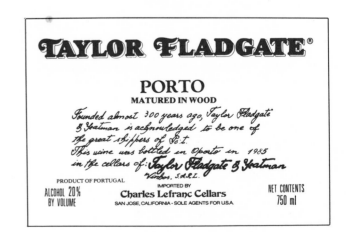

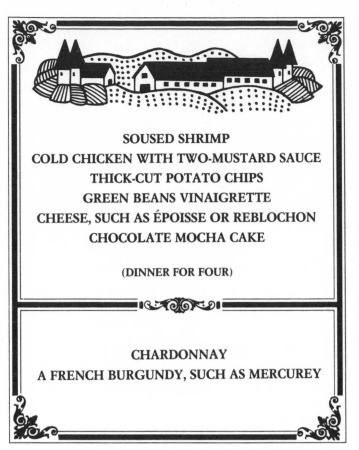

SOUSED SHRIMP
COLD CHICKEN WITH TWO-MUSTARD SAUCE
THICK-CUT POTATO CHIPS
GREEN BEANS VINAIGRETTE
CHEESE, SUCH AS ÉPOISSE OR REBLOCHON
CHOCOLATE MOCHA CAKE

(DINNER FOR FOUR)

CHARDONNAY
A FRENCH BURGUNDY, SUCH AS MERCUREY

FAMILY DINNER

A very American meal— shrimp, roast chicken, potatoes, chocolate cake—with a surprise slipped in, a fine cheese and a good red wine from France. It's also a do-ahead meal. But, to make them perfect, fry up the potatoes only at the last minute.

You have a choice here. You can serve the Chardonnay with both the shrimp and chicken. Or, if your burgundy is light and young—and Beaujolais will do as well—just chill it slightly and enjoy it with the chicken and the cheese. Red wines can work with fowl. Serve very strong iced coffee with dessert.

This menu could easily serve six. You need only roast a second chicken— and there's no harm in having leftover cold chicken. See **Recipe Index** for Green Beans Vinaigrette.

SOUSED SHRIMP

Two 12-ounce bottles or cans of beer
1 large onion, sliced thin
1 garlic clove, peeled
2 teaspoons salt
8 black peppercorns
2 bay leaves
1/2 teaspoon Tabasco sauce
2 teaspoons lemon juice
2 pounds raw shrimp, shelled and deveined

In a large pot, bring all the ingredients, except the shrimp, to a boil. Add the shrimp and cook for 2 minutes. Leave the shrimp in the cooking liquid to cool and marinate overnight in the refrigerator.

Drain and serve cold, moistening the shrimp with some of the cooking liquid; serve on individual plates, spooning a bit of the marinade on top.

COLD CHICKEN WITH TWO-MUSTARD SAUCE

MUSTARD SAUCE
4 tablespoons grainy mustard
2 tablespoons Dijon mustard
1 cup heavy cream
1/2 teaspoon lemon juice
6 drops Tabasco sauce
1/4 teaspoon Angostura bitters
1/2 teaspoon sugar

Combine the mustards in a bowl. Stir in the heavy cream; then add the remaining ingredients, mix well, and taste for seasoning. Serve at room temperature.

ROAST CHICKEN
One 3 1/2- to 4-pound chicken
1/4 pound unsalted butter, softened
Salt to taste

Preheat the oven to 375 degrees. Generously rub the entire chicken with softened butter and place a large lump inside. Place chicken on a rack in a roasting pan and roast for approximately 1 1/4 hours, basting it every 15 minutes with the pan juices.

When the chicken is brown and the drumsticks can be jiggled slightly, remove it from the oven. Lightly sprinkle with salt while the chicken is hot. Cool, but do not refrigerate. Carve into eight pieces to serve.

THICK-CUT POTATO CHIPS

6 unpeeled russet potatoes, scrubbed
Vegetable oil
3 teaspoons coarse salt

Cut the potatoes into slices 1/4 inch thick. Heat the oil in a large skillet; add the potatoes and fry until golden brown on all sides. Spread out on layers of paper towels to drain. Sprinkle with coarse salt and serve immediately.

CHOCOLATE MOCHA CAKE

CAKE
9 ounces bittersweet chocolate
1 cup milk, in all
1 cup granulated sugar
3 egg yolks
1/4 pound unsalted butter
1/2 cup packed dark brown sugar
2 cups sifted all-purpose flour
1 teaspoon baking soda
1/2 teaspoon salt
1/4 cup water
1 tablespoon vanilla extract
6 eggs whites

Preheat the oven to 375 degrees. In a saucepan over low heat, combine the chocolate with 1/2 cup of the milk. Stir until the chocolate has melted and the mixture is smooth. Blend in the granulated sugar and 1 egg yolk. Cook over low heat, stirring, until the chocolate is thick and smooth. Remove from the heat and cool.

In a bowl, cream together the butter and dark brown sugar until soft and light. Beat in the remaining egg yolks. In a separate bowl, combine the flour, baking soda, and salt. In a measuring cup, mix the remaining 1/2 cup milk with the water and vanilla.

Add the flour mixture to the butter mixture one-third at a time, alternating with the milk mixture. Then stir in the chocolate.

Beat the egg whites until stiff but not dry and fold them into the cake batter. Divide the batter between two buttered 9-inch-round layer cake pans and bake for 25 to 30 minutes, or until a cake tester comes out clean. Turn the cakes out onto wire racks to cool.

COFFEE ICING
4 tablespoons instant coffee
4 tablespoons boiling water
1/2 pound unsalted butter, softened
2 1/2 cups confectioner's sugar

Dissolve the coffee in the boiling water and then cool. With an electric mixer (to save time and energy), beat the butter and gradually add the coffee. Continue to beat, adding the confectioner's sugar. Then beat for another 2 minutes.

To assemble the cake, spread icing between the layers, and then frost the top and sides.

STRACCIATELLA
LIVER VENEZIANA
ORZO
PARMESAN AND FRUIT

(LUNCH OR SUPPER FOR SIX)

ORVIETO OR FRASCATI
BARBERA
BAROLO

WINTER LUNCH OR SUPPER

Sometimes, the most satisfying menus come from mixing ethnic origins—and sometimes just the opposite. Here's one that's pure Italian, bright and friendly. It will warm everybody up, regardless of the weather.

The wines are all Italian, too. The liver, with its vinegar and onions, wants a robust red wine, which Barbera is. The Barolo, larger than life and smooth when aged, fits hand in glove with fruit and cheese.

The whole point of the Venetian method of cooking liver is that it is done very quickly at the last minute. Get someone to cook the *orzo* for you while you do the liver.

STRACCIATELLA

2 quarts chicken broth
2 carrots
2 celery stalks
1 small onion, peeled
1/4 cup freshly grated imported Parmesan cheese
3 tablespoons finely chopped Italian parsley leaves
1/4 teaspoon ground nutmeg
4 eggs, lightly beaten

In a heavy saucepan, bring the broth to a boil. Add the carrots, celery, and onion and simmer until the vegetables are soft. Strain, pressing down hard on the solids. Return the soup to the pot.

Combine the remaining ingredients, except the eggs, and mix into the soup. (Take the Parmesan from the piece you will use for the last course.) Bring the broth to a boil. Pour in the eggs a bit at a time, stirring constantly. Continue stirring, at a simmer, for 2 or 3 minutes.

Note: *Stracciatella* translates into "little rags." This gives you an idea of the way the soup should look. Prepare the broth in advance, of course. The eggs *can* be added ahead, but this does not really accomplish much. It's simpler to finish the soup when guests are about to be seated.

LIVER VENEZIANA

1/4 pound unsalted butter
1/2 cup olive oil
3 tablespoons red wine vinegar
3 large white onions, sliced
2 pounds calf's liver, sliced into thin strips
2 tablespoons flour
3 tablespoons finely chopped Italian parsley leaves
Salt to taste
Freshly ground black pepper to taste
1 tablespoon balsamic vinegar

Heat the butter with the oil in a large skillet. Add the red wine vinegar and onions and sauté over very low heat until wilted.

Dust the strips of liver with the flour and add them to the skillet. Sauté over medium-high heat for 4 minutes, stirring constantly. Remove the liver and onions to a heated dish and add the parsley, salt, and pepper to the juices remaining in the skillet. Stir briefly, add the balsamic vinegar, and pour the mixture over the liver.

Serve the liver and onions with a helping of *orzo* alongside.

ORZO

This is the small pasta usually used in soups that substitutes so well for rice.

1 1/2 quarts water
2 teaspoons salt
2 teaspoons olive oil
3/4 pound orzo

Bring the water to a boil in a saucepan and add the salt and olive oil. Slowly pour in the *orzo,* stir, and bring back to a boil; then lower heat slightly and cook until al dente, about 5 minutes. Drain and serve immediately with the liver.

PARMESAN AND FRUIT

1 1/2 pounds imported Parmesan cheese
Basket of assorted fruit (apples, pears, grapes, etc.)

Place the cheese and fruit in the center of the table. Leave the cheese in one piece and provide your guests with sturdy short knives to cut it.

Note: Parmesan cheese keeps very well in the refrigerator. Double wrap it in wax paper and then tightly in aluminum foil.

BARBERA D'ALBA
DENOMINAZIONE D'ORIGINE CONTROLLATA
VIGNETO MESSOIRANO
1982

PRODUCED IN ITALY AND BOTTLED BY
AZIENDA AGRICOLA CANTINE DEL
CASTELLO DI NEIVE - ITALIA

IMPORTED BY
Charles Lefranc Cellars
SAN JOSE, CALIFORNIA · SOLE AGENTS FOR U.S.A.

DRY RED WINE   PRODUCE OF ITALY
NET. CONT. 750 ML (25,4 FL. OZ)   ALCOHOL 12,5% BY VOLUME

R. I. V. 5912 CN

TEQUILA TOMATO SOUP
ROASTED BEEF RIBS
MEXICAN RICE
CUCUMBER YOGURT SALAD
BLACKBERRY CUSTARD

(DINNER FOR EIGHT)

JUG RED
JUG WHITE

MEXICAN PATIO DINNER

Americans love Mexican cuisine, authentic or adapted. Here it certainly adapts to our backyard barbecue, and it adapts to wine when you don't aim too high. The tastes, textures, and colors are strong and clear and refreshingly varied. It is variety that makes this menu surprisingly sophisticated.

The English have a word for it: "plonck," by which they mean inexpensive table wine. Serve white or red, or both, and serve them icy cold: generic chablis or burgundy from California, wines from southern Italy or Corsica or Spain—wines that grow where summers are hot.

The beef ribs can be finished under a broiler rather than on an outdoor grill, so the menu can just as well be served indoors as out. We're assuming hot weather; everything but the final cooking of the ribs can be done ahead in the cool of the morning.

TEQUILA TOMATO SOUP

Three 35-ounce cans Italian plum tomatoes, with their juice
3 cups chicken broth
1/4 cup chopped fresh coriander, or to taste
1 teaspoon hot red pepper flakes
Juice of 1 lime

6 drops Tabasco sauce
1 tablespoon sugar
1 tablespoon Worcestershire sauce ·
2 teaspoons Bovril or *glace de viande* (available commercially)
1 small onion, minced
Freshly ground black pepper to taste
8 ounces (1 cup) tequila

Combine all the ingredients, except the tequila, in a saucepan and simmer for 30 minutes. Purée coarsely through a colander. Add the tequila and taste for seasoning. Cover, chill, taste again, and serve icy cold in glass bowls.

ROASTED BEEF RIBS

28 short ribs of beef

Preheat the oven to 375 degrees. Roast the ribs on a rack in a roasting pan until almost tender, about 1 or 1 1/4 hours. Remove from the oven and finish cooking on a barbecue grill for 15 to 20 minutes.

Note: If a grill is not available, finish the ribs under the broiler, close to the heat; broil for 15 minutes, turning once.

Short ribs usually are sold in 7-rib blocks as they are the bottom pieces of a 7-rib roast. You will need about 3 ribs per person. Don't hesitate to have extras; they reheat like a dream.

MEXICAN RICE

4 cups chicken broth
4 tablespoons unsalted butter
2 cups rice
1 sweet red pepper
1 sweet yellow pepper
1 green pepper
1 large onion
One 2-ounce can chile peppers, drained
One 2-ounce jar pimientos, drained
One 4-ounce jar pitted green olives, drained
One 4-ounce can pitted black olives, drained
2 tablespoons olive oil
1 teaspoon hot red pepper flakes
6 to 8 drops Tabasco sauce

Put the chicken broth in a saucepan and bring to a boil. Add the butter and let it melt. Pour in the rice, cover, and simmer until all the liquid has been absorbed, about 20 minutes.

Chop the vegetables, peppers, and olives and sauté them in the olive oil until heated through. Combine with the cooked rice and add the pepper flakes and Tabasco sauce.

Note: This can be made ahead and reheated in a microwave oven.

CUCUMBER YOGURT SALAD

3 seedless English cucumbers, peeled and thinly
    sliced
1 large Bermuda onion, peeled and minced
4 cups plain yogurt
1 tablespoon dried coriander
1 tablespoon sugar
1 teaspoon ground cumin
1/2 teaspoon salt
1 tablespoon lemon juice

Combine all the ingredients in a bowl. Toss, cover, and
chill.

BLACKBERRY CUSTARD

CUSTARD
3/4 cup sugar
2 tablespoons cornstarch
1/8 teaspoon salt
1 1/2 cups milk
1 1/2 cups heavy cream
6 egg yolks, well beaten
2 tablespoons unsalted butter
1 1/2 teaspoons vanilla extract
1 cup whipping cream
1 cup blackberries

In the top of a double boiler, combine the sugar, cornstarch, and salt. Combine the milk and cream and
gradually stir this mixture into the dry ingredients. Cover
and cook over barely simmering water without boiling for
8 minutes. Uncover, stir, and cook for about 10 minutes
longer. Stir in the egg yolks and butter and cook for another 2 minutes, stirring occasionally. Let cool, stirring
occasionally; then add the vanilla.

Whip the cream and combine it with the berries; then
fold into the custard. Serve in glass bowls and top with
the blackberry sauce.

BLACKBERRY SAUCE
3 pint baskets blackberries
2 tablespoons dry vermouth
Peel of 1 lemon cut into very fine julienne strips
1 tablespoon sugar, or more to taste

Press the blackberries through a sieve into a bowl. Add
the remaining ingredients and taste for sweetness.

Note: You can substitute raspberries. You can also use
frozen berries for the sauce; if so, first defrost them completely. Taste. There will probably be too much sugar, so
you will need to add lemon—with caution.

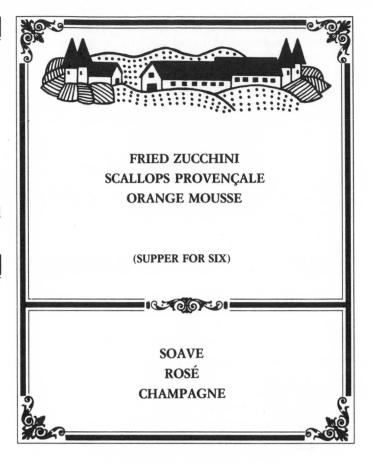

FRIED ZUCCHINI
SCALLOPS PROVENÇALE
ORANGE MOUSSE

(SUPPER FOR SIX)

SOAVE
ROSÉ
CHAMPAGNE

SUMMER SUPPER

A festive small menu that is easy enough to do during the week.

The first wine should be light, in keeping with the season and the delicate nature of the vegetable. The tendency is to think white wine with scallops and red with the flavorful sauce. Both instincts are right, but in this case a crisp, well-chilled rosé from Provence or California (rosé of Cabernet, for example) is not a compromise but the right choice. Seek out a demi-sec or "dry" sparkling wine from California or Italy to match with the mousse, and place a slice of orange peel in each glass before pouring.

Brief and careful cooking is what makes the recipes in this menu work. Use it when you have guests who enjoy knowing what you're doing and how you're doing it, uninvolved though it is. Serving six is the convenient maximum number. The zucchini and scallop recipes are easily cut back for four or two.

FRIED ZUCCHINI

2 eggs
1/4 cup milk
Freshly ground white pepper to taste
1 1/2 cups dry bread crumbs
3/4 cup grated Romano or Parmesan cheese
2 tablespoons minced fresh parsley
3 large zucchini, cut into slices 1/2 inch thick
3/4 cup olive oil

Lightly beat together the eggs, milk, and white pepper in a bowl. Combine the bread crumbs with the grated cheese and parsley and mix well. Dip each slice of zucchini into the egg mixture and then into the bread crumbs.

Heat the oil in a large skillet and pan-fry (in two batches, if necessary) until golden brown, about 1 minute on each side. Drain on a baking sheet lined with paper towels; the zucchini can be kept hot in a 250-degree oven. Serve hot on a warm platter lined with a kitchen towel or napkin.

Note: The zucchini should be coated and cooked just before serving, but the ingredients can be prepared ahead.

SCALLOPS PROVENCALE

PROVENÇALE TOMATO SAUCE
One 35-ounce can Italian plum tomatoes
1 teaspoon Pernod
1 teaspoon dried fennel seeds
12 julienne strips lemon peel
15 julienne strips orange peel
1 tablespoon dried tarragon
1 tablespoon dried basil
1/4 teaspoon hot red pepper flakes
1/4 cup dry vermouth
1 small bunch Italian parsley, stems removed,
    chopped

Drain the tomatoes well, chop them coarsely, and put them in a sauté pan. Add remaining ingredients and cook for 15 to 20 minutes over medium heat, stirring occasionally. Set aside and warm before using.

SCALLOPS
5 tablespoons unsalted butter
3 pounds scallops (if large, cut them in half)
3 tablespoons dry vermouth
Freshly ground white pepper to taste

In a large skillet over medium heat, melt the butter and heat to a sizzle. Add the scallops, vermouth, and white pepper. Stir until heated through, about 4 minutes. The scallops are ready when no longer transparent.

Add the warmed Provençale sauce to the scallops and heat together for 1 or 2 minutes. Taste and add salt if desired.

In accord with the informality of the evening, bring the cooking pan with the scallops to the dining room. This helps them stay warm and means one less serving dish to wash.

Notes: The sauce can be made at any point in advance, even frozen. (It is an excellent sauce for pasta.) If you want a more refined sauce, strain it before combining it with the scallops.

ORANGE MOUSSE

8 eggs, separated
1/4 cup sugar
2 tablespoons orange liqueur
1/8 teaspoon orange extract
1/4 cup fresh orange juice
1 cup whipping cream
1 teaspoon vanilla extract
Julienne strips from the peel of 1 orange

In the top of a double boiler, over barely simmering water, combine the egg yolks, sugar, liqueur, orange extract, and orange juice. Beat until thick and foamy, about 15 minutes. Transfer to a bowl and leave at room temperature until cool.

Beat the egg whites until soft peaks form. In another bowl, combine the cream and vanilla and beat until soft peaks form. Fold the egg whites into the egg-yolk base; then fold in the whipped cream.

Spoon into individual wine glasses, top with the orange peel, and chill until time to serve. (The mousse is too frothy to be easily spooned from a bowl.)

Note: The mousse should be finished and refrigerated shortly before the arrival of the guests. You want to hold it the shortest time possible.

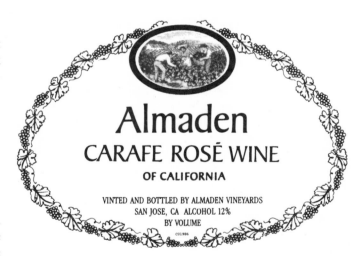

Almaden
CARAFE ROSÉ WINE
OF CALIFORNIA

VINTED AND BOTTLED BY ALMADEN VINEYARDS
SAN JOSE, CA ALCOHOL 12%
BY VOLUME

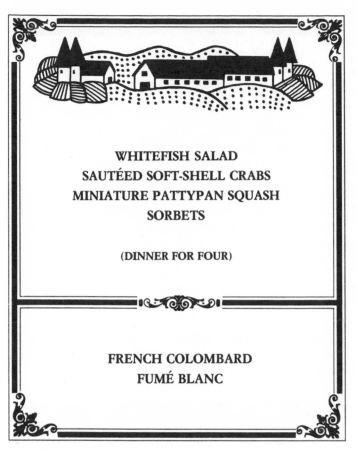

WHITEFISH SALAD
SAUTÉED SOFT-SHELL CRABS
MINIATURE PATTYPAN SQUASH
SORBETS

(DINNER FOR FOUR)

FRENCH COLOMBARD
FUMÉ BLANC

EASY STYLISH DINNER

The plot here is to think of just the right ingredients so that it's possible to serve an impressive dinner by doing almost nothing. If this meal takes more than 20 minutes advance preparation and a 10 minute cooking time, you're doing something wrong.

The wines are naturals with seafood. The Colombard will complement the smoky flavor of the salad, and the slightly flinty Fumé Blanc is what the crab requires—or you could go for a Pouilly-Fumé for the same effect.

The menu can easily enough be multiplied to serve more people, but this will slow you down a bit; there's a limit to how many crabs will fit in one layer in a skillet, so they would have to be cooked in batches.

For dessert, buy the best fresh fruit sorbets available—an assortment of two or even three. Use a small ice-cream scoop to serve one of each in glass dessert bowls and pass a plate of crisp little cookies.

WHITEFISH SALAD

3/4 cup mayonnaise
1 red onion, finely diced
1/2 teaspoon lemon juice
3 drops Tabasco sauce
1 tablespoon chopped parsley
2 large smoked whitefish, skinned, boned, and cut into bite-size pieces
8 or more perfect Boston lettuce leaves

In a bowl, mix together the mayonnaise, onion, and seasonings. Gently combine the dressing with the fish.

On individual plates, place equal amounts of the salad on lettuce leaves and serve with thinly sliced black bread, buttered or not, as you wish.

SAUTEED SOFT-SHELL CRABS

1 cup flour
1/2 teaspoon cayenne pepper
1/2 teaspoon salt
8 medium-size soft-shell crabs
1/4 pound unsalted butter
2 tablespoons lemon juice

Combine the flour, cayenne, and salt, and dip the crabs in the seasoned flour. Over medium-high heat, sauté them in the butter in a large skillet until brown, about 2 to 3 minutes on each side. Remove the crabs to a platter and add the lemon juice to the pan juices. Stir and pour the juices over the crabs.

MINIATURE PATTYPAN SQUASH

8 miniature pattypan squash
2 tablespoons unsalted butter, melted
Salt and freshly ground white pepper to taste

Steam the squash until tender, about 20 minutes. Coat them with butter to give them a shine and season with salt and pepper. Serve whole.

Note: Slices of summer squash would be good, too, though not as subtle. It's worth noting that expensive miniature vegetables are not always as fresh in the market as they should be; use your judgment.

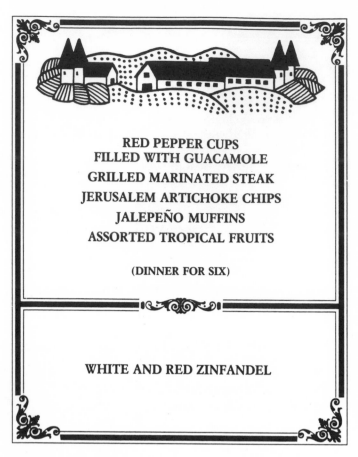

RED PEPPER CUPS
FILLED WITH GUACAMOLE

GRILLED MARINATED STEAK

JERUSALEM ARTICHOKE CHIPS

JALEPEÑO MUFFINS

ASSORTED TROPICAL FRUITS

(DINNER FOR SIX)

WHITE AND RED ZINFANDEL

CASUAL SUMMER MEAL

As anyone from the South-west will tell you, hot weather calls for spicy food. If you were summering in Santa Fe with friends, they'd offer you a meal like this. Our version is not exotic, the better to accommodate a hot day wherever you may be.

🍷 Strong flavors call for robust wines. That's what you get from Zinfandels. Chill them, definitely, both the red and the white, and let your guests choose. For those who choose red, bring another glass for the white to drink with the fruit.

🍴 Nothing formal is going on here, but the menu begs for a division of labor. One person will deal with the Jerusalem artichokes and the muffins while another cooks the steaks, preferably on an outdoor grill. The cool guacamole cups and the dessert are ready ahead, though not too far ahead. One of the nice things about being a guest is having ripe fresh fruit presented to you cut up and ready to eat.

RED PEPPER CUPS FILLED WITH GUACAMOLE

6 small sweet red peppers
3 ripe avocados
1/2 cup chopped fresh coriander
1/4 cup minced onion
1 tablespoon lemon juice
1 teaspoon salt
1/2 cup peeled, seeded, and chopped tomato
1 tablespoon chopped jalepeño peppers

Remove the tops and seeds of the red peppers and cut a small sliver off the bottoms so they will stand upright. Remove avocado pulp from shell and mash the flesh coarsely with a fork. Combine with the remaining ingredients and taste for seasoning. Divide the guacamole equally among the peppers. Replace their tops and refrigerate for no more than 1 hour. Serve cold.

Note: These are best made as close to serving time as possible. If you're already tired of seeing peppers and guacamole at cocktail buffets, it's because they sit there too long. They're delicious made freshly at home. Don't forget to provide small knives for each guest.

GRILLED MARINATED STEAK

1/2 cup olive oil
1 cup red wine
1 tablespoon hot red pepper flakes
1 small bunch parsley, minced
1 small onion, minced
2 flank steaks

Combine the oil, wine, hot pepper flakes, parsley, and onion in a bowl. Divide the marinade between two plastic bags and place one flank steak in each. Close the bags tightly and put them in a shallow pan. (This guards against spillage.) Let the steaks marinate overnight in the refrigerator, turning the bags occasionally.

Bring the steaks to room temperature and wipe off before broiling or grilling. For rare, cook for 3 or 4 minutes on each side, close to the heat. To serve, slice very thin on the diagonal.

Note: If using an outdoor grill, the coals should be very hot, with an ashy glow, before the steaks are put on to cook.

JERUSALEM ARTICHOKE CHIPS

1 1/2 pounds unpeeled Jerusalem artichokes, scrubbed
Vegetable oil
4 teaspoons coarse salt

As you would with thick potato chips, cut the artichokes into 1/4-inch slices and deep-fry them in hot vegetable oil until crunchy and golden brown. Spread out on paper towels to drain. Sprinkle with coarse salt and serve warm.

JALEPENO MUFFINS

2 cups yellow cornmeal
1 cup all-purpose flour
2 teaspoons baking powder
1/4 teaspoon salt
1/4 cup sugar
3 tablespoons chopped jalepeño peppers
1 garlic clove, crushed
1 egg, lightly beaten
1 cup milk
2 tablespoons unsalted butter, melted

Preheat the oven to 425 degrees. Butter muffin tins generously.

Combine the cornmeal, flour, baking powder, salt, sugar, peppers, and garlic in a bowl. In a separate bowl, combine the egg, milk, and butter. Pour this mixture into the dry ingredients and mix well. Fill the individual muffin cups two thirds full with the batter and bake until golden brown, about 20 minutes.

Note: The recipe yields twelve 3-inch muffins.

ASSORTED TROPICAL FRUITS

Fruits, such as kiwi, papaya, mango, star fruit
6 mint sprigs for garnish

Peel the fruits and cut them into slices or wedges. Arrange them on individual plates and refrigerate, covered with plastic wrap. Decorate with mint and serve with small sugar cookies.

Note: The plates can be arranged ahead, but best not more than 2 or 3 hours.

PUMPKIN SOUP
POACHED TURKEY BREAST
DUXELLES DRESSING
BUTTERED BROCCOLI
APPLE CRUMBLE WITH HEAVY CREAM

(DINNER FOR TEN TO TWELVE)

JOHANNISBERG RIESLING
LIGHT ZINFANDEL
SPARKLING VOUVRAY

HOLIDAY OCCASION

There is a reason why traditional meals become traditional—people love them. This special-occasion menu, with its echoes of the past, presents old favorites in new ways; it's both fresh and sure to please. It also benefits from preparation in advance.

"Dry" Riesling (which is slightly sweet) is a perfect complement to the cream and spices in the soup. The mushrooms, not the turkey, are the dominant flavor in the main course, so a full-bodied red is appropriate and also gives the turkey a lift. A soft sparkling wine with a little sweetness goes well with an apple dessert and is likely to please everyone.

Note that literally every course here is made ahead and ready to reheat before serving. It will be calmer in the kitchen if you allow only one guest to help reheat and serve the main course. Assign someone else to pour the wines.

PUMPKIN SOUP

1 bunch leeks, white part only, chopped fine
8 tablespoons unsalted butter, in all
Six 16-ounce cans unsweetened pumpkin purée
4 cups light cream
2 cups chicken broth
1 cup heavy cream
1 cup rice
2 tablespoons sugar
1 teaspoon Tabasco sauce

1/4 teaspoon ground cinnamon
1/4 teaspoon ground nutmeg
1/4 teaspoon lemon juice
Salt and freshly ground white pepper to taste
2 cups pumpkin seeds

In a soup pot, sauté the leeks in 6 tablespoons of the butter until soft. Add all the remaining ingredients, except the pumpkin seeds. Stir well. Simmer for 30 minutes. The rice should be completely soft.

In a food processor, purée the soup in batches, then sieve if not perfectly smooth. Reheat just before serving.

Sauté the pumpkin seeds in the remaining 2 tablespoons of butter until crisp. Drain well on paper towels. Pass separately at the table.

POACHED TURKEY BREAST

3 quarts chicken stock
2 carrots, chopped roughly
2 celery stalks, chopped roughly
1 bunch parsley sprigs
1 medium-size onion, chopped roughly
8 black peppercorns
One 10- to 12-pound whole boned turkey breast, with skin on

In a large, deep roasting pan, combine all the ingredients, except the turkey, and boil until the vegetables are soft. Submerge turkey breast in the boiling stock and simmer for 15 minutes. Turn off the heat, cover, and set aside until the liquid cools. Remove the turkey, take off the skin, and discard the vegetables. Return the turkey to the stock and reheat it in the stock shortly before serving.

Slice the turkey against the grain into thin slices, arrange on a platter, and spoon a little hot stock on top.

Note: Although the meat will be just slightly pink, it will be fully cooked.

DUXELLES DRESSING

2 pounds mushrooms, chopped fine
1/4 pound unsalted butter
1/2 cup dry vermouth
1/4 cup brandy
1 teaspoon lemon juice
3 tablespoons chopped fresh parsley
2 tablespoons chopped fresh tarragon
1 teaspoon dried basil
1 teaspoon dried chervil
1/2 teaspoon dried thyme
3 cups dry bread crumbs
1 teaspoon salt
Freshly ground black pepper and Tabasco sauce to taste

In a large skillet, sauté the mushrooms in the butter until all their juices are released, about 5 minutes (depending on their moisture content). Add all the liquids and herbs. Cook over a low heat for about 15 minutes. (Add finely chopped sautéed turkey giblets and/or chopped ham if you wish.) Slowly stir in the bread crumbs 1 cup at a time, until the mixture is fluffy. Season with salt, pepper, and Tabasco to taste. Serve warm.

Notes: The dressing should be dark and rich. If there are leftovers, this dressing can serve many uses (for sandwiches, in stuffed tomatoes). It reheats well in the oven (covered) and the microwave oven. If it turns a bit dry, top with a few strips of bacon before reheating, or dot with butter.

BUTTERED BROCCOLI

6 bunches fresh broccoli (about 3/4 pound per person before trimming)
2 tablespoons unsalted butter
8 black peppercorns
Salt and freshly ground white pepper to taste

Trim broccoli well; then cut into attractive stalks, and rinse well. Blanch the broccoli with the peppercorns in boiling water for 8 to 10 minutes, or until crisp-tender. Immediately plunge into cold water; drain thoroughly.

Melt the butter in a stove-to-table casserole. Turn off the heat. Add the broccoli and toss until coated. Cover and set aside. Reheat just before serving, seasoning with salt and pepper.

APPLE CRUMBLE WITH HEAVY CREAM

4 1/2 pounds tart apples (Granny Smiths), peeled and sliced
1/4 cup brandy
Juice and grated rind of 1 lemon
2 cups light brown sugar, in all
1 tablespoon vanilla extract
1 tablespoon ground ginger
1/2 teaspoon ground nutmeg
1/2 teaspoon ground cinnamon
1/2 pound unsalted butter, in all
2 cups all-purpose flour
1/2 teaspoon salt
8 cups heavy cream

Preheat the oven to 350 degrees.

In a large bowl, combine the apples with the brandy, lemon juice and rind, 1 cup of the brown sugar, vanilla, ginger, nutmeg, and cinnamon. Generously butter a large oven-to-table baking dish and fill with the apple mixture.

Combine the remaining brown sugar and the flour, and salt in a bowl. Cut in the butter until the mixture forms pea-size crumbs. Sprinkle the crumbs evenly over the apples. Bake until the top is golden brown and the apple mixture is bubbly, about 40 minutes. Remove and set aside. Reheat in a 300-degree oven shortly before serving. Serve lukewarm, with heavy cream to pour over.

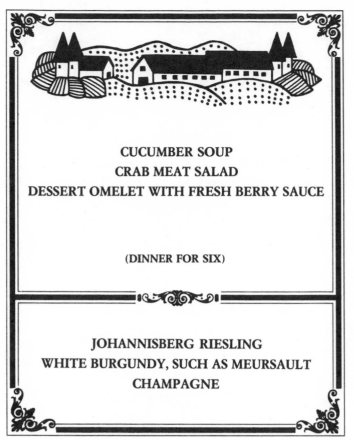

CUCUMBER SOUP
CRAB MEAT SALAD
DESSERT OMELET WITH FRESH BERRY SAUCE

(DINNER FOR SIX)

JOHANNISBERG RIESLING
WHITE BURGUNDY, SUCH AS MEURSAULT
CHAMPAGNE

SUMMER SEAFOOD DINNER

When the dog days descend, if the very thought of food becomes oppressive, think color. This summer dinner menu is expressly designed to refresh the mind and the palate. It warms up at the end after coolness at the beginning.

Cucumbers relate very well to Riesling wines, whether from Germany's Rheingau or California. Choose one that is not very dry, even a Spätlese. The crab meat salad is a rich dish that wants a rich wine for company. Meursault fills the bill very well, as will a fruity California Chardonnay. The omelet is light and airy, so any Champagne, even a very dry one, will be compatible. For a festive touch, place one of the same berries you use for the sauce in each glass.

Many of the menus in this book suggest wine with dessert—not something every American household is used to. Yet it is the simplest of luxuries to provide. In due course, at the end of this otherwise entirely do-ahead meal, the prospect of a specially chosen bubbly will impel you back to the kitchen to produce the frothy omelet to accompany it.

3 pounds cucumbers, peeled and cut into large chunks
2 quarts chicken broth
1 small onion, quartered
1 large bunch fresh dill, stems removed
3 tablespoons farina (Cream of Wheat)
2 tablespoons white wine vinegar
1 cup sour cream
Salt and freshly ground white pepper to taste
Cucumber slices and chopped dill for garnish

Put the cucumbers in a heavy saucepan. Add the chicken broth (the cucumbers should be three-quarters covered), onion, dill, farina, and vinegar. Cover partially, bring to a boil, and simmer until the cucumbers are soft and mushy, 20 to 30 minutes. When done, purée in a food processor, food mill, or blender.

Strain the soup through a colander or large-holed sieve into a bowl. Combine the soup and sour cream by first mixing a bit of the soup, a tablespoon at a time, into the sour cream until it is of the same consistency as the soup. Check the thickness; it should be the consistency of vichyssoise. Add more chicken broth to thin, if necessary.

Taste for seasoning; then add any of the following to taste: chopped dill, white pepper, salt, white wine vinegar, sour cream. The soup should be pale green, with flecks of dill throughout. Cover, chill, and taste again.

Serve at the table from a chilled tureen. Garnish with thin cucumber slices and pass extra chopped dill.

Notes: The soup can be made a day ahead. It can also be served hot. Reheat to serve, but do not boil or the sour cream will curdle.

2 egg yolks
2 cups mayonnaise
2 tablespoons snipped fresh chives
2 tablespoons olive oil
1 teaspoon lemon juice, or more to taste
Pinch of cayenne pepper
Tabasco sauce to taste
2 1/2 to 3 pounds crabmeat (lump, Alaskan king crab legs, or the best canned crab), picked over
Assortment of bitter greens
Sweet yellow and red peppers

Beat the egg yolks into the mayonnaise. Add the chives, olive oil, lemon juice, cayenne pepper, and Tabasco sauce. Combine this sauce with the crab. (For a tighter salad, use less mayonnaise.)

Place the crab meat salad on individual plates (this allows you to make an equitable distribution of the salad and a pretty arrangement of each portion). Surround with a mixture of slightly bitter greens, such as arugula, radicchio, lamb's lettuce, red leaf lettuce. Garnish with thin strips of yellow and red peppers.

Note: The crab meat should be prepared the same day you serve it, in the morning if you wish. If there are leftovers, do not let them languish more than a day in the refrigerator.

DESSERT OMELET WITH FRESH BERRY SAUCE

2 pint baskets strawberries, blackberries, or raspberries (you could use frozen berries)
1 tablespoon rum, Cognac, or orange liqueur
8 eggs, separated
2 tablespoons granulated sugar
2 teaspoons vanilla extract
3 tablespoons unsalted butter
Sprinkle of confectioner's sugar

Press 1 1/4 baskets of the berries into a bowl through a sieve to remove seeds; reserve 3/4 basket for topping. Stir in the liquor. Cover and chill.

Preheat the oven to 375 degrees. Beat the egg whites until soft peaks form. Mix together the egg yolks, granulated sugar, and vanilla extract and beat until thick and lemon-yellow. Combine, folding the egg whites into the yolks.

In a skillet with a heatproof handle, melt the butter over medium heat. Pour in the egg mixture and cook on top of the stove until set on the bottom. (The mixture is thick and needs only a bit of lifting from the bottom and pushing from the sides for even cooking). *Do not fold.* Sprinkle the top with confectioner's sugar. Transfer to the oven and bake until puffy and brown, about 15 minutes.

To serve, cut into wedges. It's a nice touch if the dessert comes to the table in its cooking pan and is sliced and passed there. Have the sauce in a pretty boat or bowl and spoon some on each plate first for a French nouvelle touch. Top each slice with the remaining berries, sliced or whole. Pass the sauceboat after serving.

Notes: Make the sauce ahead. The eggs for the omelet should be separated before company arrives and left, covered, at room temperature.

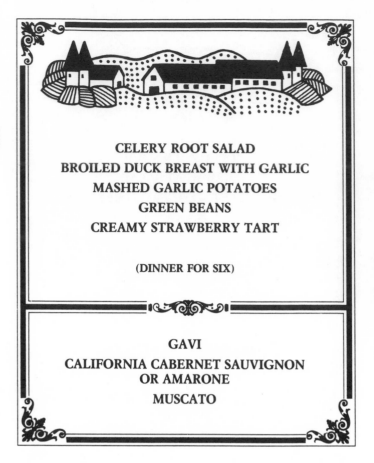

CELERY ROOT SALAD
BROILED DUCK BREAST WITH GARLIC
MASHED GARLIC POTATOES
GREEN BEANS
CREAMY STRAWBERRY TART

(DINNER FOR SIX)

GAVI
CALIFORNIA CABERNET SAUVIGNON
OR AMARONE
MUSCATO

DINNER FROM THE RIVIERA

The sort of earthy yet glamorous meal you might expect on the terrace of a small hotel overlooking the Mediterranean: a country-style French—but very chic—duck dish and a light, pretty dessert.

The wines are international. Gavi is a Riviera favorite; it *will* work with the celery root salad—not a dish exactly "meant" for wine. The duck and potatoes need a red wine with strong texture and flavor. Finish with something light and not too serious.

Only the duck is cooked at the last minute. The garlic potatoes can be made an hour or so ahead and reheated. The best beans, if you can find them, would be French *haricots verts*.

CELERY ROOT SALAD

Juice of 1 lemon
3 medium-size celery roots, peeled
3 tablespoons red wine vinegar
3/4 cup olive oil
Salt and freshly ground white pepper to taste
2 tablespoons chopped fresh Italian parsley leaves
3 medium-size tomatoes, halved and sliced thin

Squeeze lemon juice into a bowl of water. Cut the celery roots into small julienne strips, placing them immediately in the water. Drain the celery and roll in a clean towel to dry. Toss with the vinegar, oil, salt and pepper, and parsley. Marinate for several hours and taste for seasoning.

To serve, place the celery root salad on individual plates and surround with the tomato slices

Note: Like potatoes, celery root must be held in acidulated water to avoid darkening until it is dressed. The julienne strips should be slim and even; a food processor helps.

BROILED DUCK BREAST WITH GARLIC

4 whole duck breasts, boned and split in half
2 garlic cloves, cut into thin slices

Remove the tendons from the underside of each duck breast. Trim the breasts so that they are evenly shaped. Make diagonal cuts into the skin (not the flesh) and insert the garlic slices into the cuts. Preheat the broiler. Place the duck breasts on a rack in a shallow pan and broil them close to the flame until the skin is brown, about 8 minutes.

Notes: We suggest you prepare 4 whole duck breasts in case someone wants an extra piece. Duck breasts will reheat beautifully without overcooking in a microwave oven, though they will lose their crispness.

Duck freezes well. See page 94 for a recipe to use the duck legs and thighs.

MASHED GARLIC POTATOES

6 medium-size boiling potatoes, peeled
4 garlic cloves, cut into thin slices
2 cups heavy cream
1/4 pound unsalted butter
1/2 teaspoon lemon juice
Pinch of cayenne pepper
Salt and freshly ground white pepper to taste

Boil together the potatoes and the garlic until the potatoes are soft. Put both through a ricer. Beat in cream and butter a little at a time. Season with the lemon juice, cayenne pepper, and salt and white pepper.

GREEN BEANS

1 1/2 pounds green beans, ends trimmed
8 black peppercorns
4 tablespoons unsalted butter
Salt and freshly ground white pepper to taste

Blanch green beans with the peppercorns in boiling water until tender but still crisp, 8 to 10 minutes. Immediately plunge into cold water to set the color. Drain the beans.

In a saucepan, melt the butter. Turn off the heat, add the green beans, and toss until coated. Cover and set aside. Reheat while you broil the duck and season with salt and pepper.

CREAMY STRAWBERRY TART

One baked 9-inch pastry shell (see Note)
Two 8-ounce packages cream cheese, softened
1 cup half-and-half
2 tablespoons sugar
1 1/2 teaspoons lemon juice, in all
2 pint baskets strawberries, hulled
1 teaspoon orange liqueur
5 ounces red currant jelly

Whip together the cream cheese, half-and-half, sugar, and 1/2 teaspoon of the lemon juice until fluffy. Spread this mixture on the bottom of the pastry shell and stand the whole strawberries on it, placing them very close together.

Melt the jelly along with the remaining teaspoon of lemon juice and the liqueur and drizzle it over the top. Refrigerate.

Serve cold and slice the tart at the table.

Note: Make a 9-inch pastry shell with your favorite short crust recipe and bake it blind.

AZIENDA AGRICOLA
La Chiara
GAVI
Net. Cont. 750 Ml.
Alchool 11,5% by vol.
DENOMINAZIONE DI ORIGINE CONTROLLATA
WHITE TABLE WINE
PRODUCED IN ITALY AND BOTTLED BY
AZIENDA AGRICOLA **LA CHIARA** DI NANDO BERGAGLIO
GAVI · ITALIA
PRODUCT OF ITALY
Charles Lefranc Cellars
Imported by
SAN JOSE, CALIFORNIA · SOLE AGENTS FOR U.S.A.

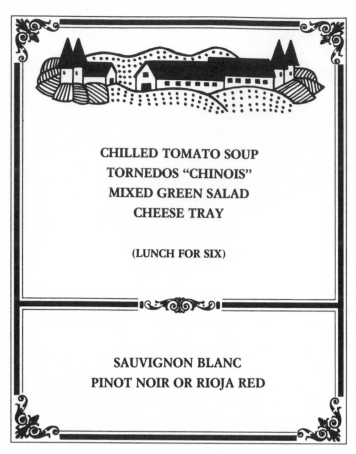

**CHILLED TOMATO SOUP
TORNEDOS "CHINOIS"
MIXED GREEN SALAD
CHEESE TRAY**

(LUNCH FOR SIX)

**SAUVIGNON BLANC
PINOT NOIR OR RIOJA RED**

WEEKEND LUNCH

The trick to this meal is the beef. It looks and tastes complicated, but it is no problem to prepare. You can even cook the meat and mushrooms early and reheat them together in a microwave oven.

The Sauvignon Blanc should have the fullness to balance the acidity in the tomato soup. Chill it well before serving. The Pinot Noir is a natural with the beef—rich enough but not overpowering to the complex flavors of the recipe.

For the chilled tomato soup, see Tequila Tomato Soup in the Recipe Index. For this menu, omit the tequila. Two thirds of the recipe will be enough, and adjust seasonings to taste.

The Pinot Noir will be agreeable to a Pont l'Évêque, a chèvre, a Saint-André. Serve water biscuits with the cheeses. No dessert today; pass chocolate truffles with coffee.

TORNEDOS "CHINOIS"

6 tournedos of beef
1 1/2 cups Dutch soy sauce (or regular soy sauce plus 1/4 cup sugar)
1 garlic clove, mashed
1/2 cup coarsely ground black pepper
1/4 pound unsalted butter
1/4 cup olive oil
1 1/2 pounds white mushrooms, stemmed or not, as you wish, and sliced thin
1/2 cup brandy
6 slices good white bread, crusts removed, halved diagonally, and toasted

Have the butcher cut the tournedos about 1 1/2 inches thick from the center of a beef tenderloin.

Put the soy sauce and garlic in a glass or earthenware dish. Encrust both sides of each tournedo with the pepper, pressing it into the meat. Lay them in the soy sauce and leave to marinate at room temperature for 2 hours, turning once midway. Remove the meat and reserve the marinade.

In a large heavy skillet, bring the butter and oil to a sizzle. Sauté the tournedos over high heat for 3 minutes on each side for rare. When done, remove the meat and add the mushrooms to the pan juices; sauté until softened. Add the reserved marinade and then add the brandy and flame it, or continue cooking until all the alcohol has been evaporated.

Return the steaks to the skillet and reheat briefly, basting constantly with the mushroom-soy mixture. To serve, place the tournedos on the toast on individual plates and top with the mushrooms and pan juices.

MIXED GREEN SALAD

1 head Boston lettuce
2 heads Bibb lettuce
A bitter green (arugula, chicory, watercress), to taste

DRESSING
3/4 cup olive oil
3 tablespoons sherry vinegar
2 tablespoons minced fresh tarragon
1/4 teaspoon dry mustard
1 teaspoon salt
3 drops Tabasco sauce
Squeeze of lemon juice
Freshly ground black pepper to taste

Combine all ingredients and mix well. Let the dressing stand for at least 1 hour. Taste for seasoning. For more tartness, add more lemon juice, not vinegar. Dress the greens just before serving.

Note: Although we usually prefer to serve salad as a separate course, serving this salad, on separate plates, along with the meat is appropriate.

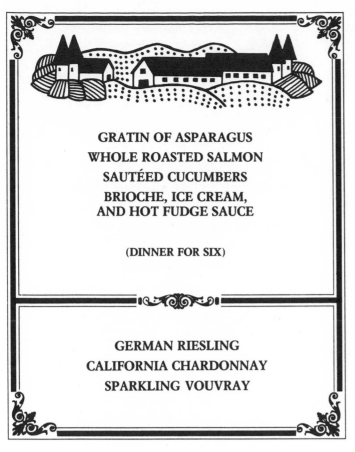

GRATIN OF ASPARAGUS

WHOLE ROASTED SALMON

SAUTÉED CUCUMBERS

BRIOCHE, ICE CREAM,
AND HOT FUDGE SAUCE

(DINNER FOR SIX)

GERMAN RIESLING
CALIFORNIA CHARDONNAY
SPARKLING VOUVRAY

SUMMER PARTY

A refined, sophisticated dinner, until you get to the extravagant adolescent dessert. A perfect menu for adults who are young at heart, and all the recipes are on the really easy side.

Wine buffs are fond of saying nothing goes well with asparagus; they're wrong, though it does depend on how the asparagus is presented. The light and delicately fruity freshness of a German Riesling really works with this recipe. The Chardonnay can be from California or France (a white Burgundy, such as Meursault), take your pick. There is no perfect solution to the problem of wine with chocolate. A sparkling wine that dances delightfully on the tongue is best—though it need not be as fine as a Vouvray.

If your broiler also heats your oven, it will be preheated when you remove the asparagus, but be sure the oven temperature is 450 degrees as specified when you put in the salmon. It can roast while the first course is served, but don't push your luck; timing is of the essence. Better for guests to wait than to start the roasting too soon and overcook the fish.

The best presentation for a roasted fish is in its roasting pan. The process is so simple, it could become a favorite recipe—worth getting a long, narrow, oval baking dish especially for fish that looks well coming from stove to table.

GRATIN OF ASPARAGUS

3 pounds large asparagus, peeled
3/4 pound ham, sliced very thin (see Note)
Unsalted butter
1 1/2 cups shredded Italian Fontina cheese
Freshly ground black pepper to taste

Blanch the asparagus in boiling salted water until just crisp-tender, about 8 minutes. Plunge them immediately into cold water. Drain and pat dry. Wrap each stalk in a piece of ham.

Lightly butter 6 individual oval ovenproof dishes. Divide the wrapped stalks equally among the dishes. Sprinkle the shredded cheese and a generous amount of black pepper evenly on top. Just before serving, broil until the cheese melts.

Notes: For the ham, use the tender Black Forest or a domestic Westphalian (imported would be too strong). The ham will insulate the asparagus and prevent overcooking. If you use smaller asparagus, wrap 2 or 3 together.

All the asparagus can be broiled in one baking dish; just be sure in advance that they will fit comfortably in one layer. If your broiler will hold the six individual dishes, they simplify serving.

WHOLE ROASTED SALMON

One 6-pound salmon, cleaned, with head and tail on
1 cup dry vermouth or white wine
1 medium-size onion, sliced thin
12 black peppercorns

Preheat the oven to 425 degrees. Oil a roasting pan well. Pour in the vermouth or wine, spread the slices of onion over the bottom, add the peppercorns, and put in the salmon. Measure the thickness of the salmon at its widest point. Roast for 8 minutes per inch, basting occasionally with the pan juices.

Note: The Canadian method for cooking fish calls for 10 minutes per inch. I prefer 8 minutes when dealing with salmon.

SAUTEED CUCUMBERS

3 seedless English cucumbers, peeled
6 tablespoons unsalted butter
1/2 cup sherry vinegar
2 tablespoons sugar
6 drops Tabasco sauce
1 teaspoon salt
3/4 teaspoon freshly ground white pepper
1/4 teaspoon cayenne pepper
Enough stemmed fresh dill to make 1/2 cup finely chopped

Cut the cucumbers into pieces 1/4 inch thick. Sauté them along with the remaining ingredients in the butter and vinegar and stir well. Cook until the cucumbers are warmed through and slightly translucent, about 6 minutes. Taste for seasoning and serve warm.

Note: sautéed cucumbers should be prepared just before serving. They do not reheat well. You can, however, cut up the cucumbers and have the other ingredients ready in advance. Start cooking them when you know the salmon has only a few more minutes more to go in the oven.

BRIOCHE, ICE CREAM, AND HOT FUDGE SAUCE

1/2 pound semisweet chocolate, coarsely chopped
   (see Note)
6 tablespoons unsalted butter
2 egg yolks, well beaten
6 breakfast-size brioche
2 pints best quality "French" vanilla ice cream

Melt the chocolate and the butter in the top of a double boiler over barely simmering water. When the mixture is smooth and glossy, combine it with the beaten egg yolks by first mixing a bit of the chocolate, drop by drop, into the egg yolks until they are the same temperature as the chocolate mixture. Then you can combine both together, a small amount at a time.

Cut off and reserve the top third of each brioche, hollow out part of the inside, fill with a scoop of ice cream (using an ice-cream scoop that will make a neat fit in the brioche), and replace the top. Freeze the ice-cream-filled brioche, first wrapping them very well in plastic wrap. To serve, let the brioche defrost in the refrigerator until the ice cream has softened. Pass the warmed chocolate sauce in a sauceboat.

Notes: The wonder of this sauce hinges on the quality of the chocolate; don't cut corners here. If the sauce is too thick, stir in 1 tablespoon of heavy cream at a time to thin. It keeps well in the refrigerator, but turns completely solid. Reheat gently to serve.

You don't have to use vanilla ice cream, but avoid any with an intrusive flavor.

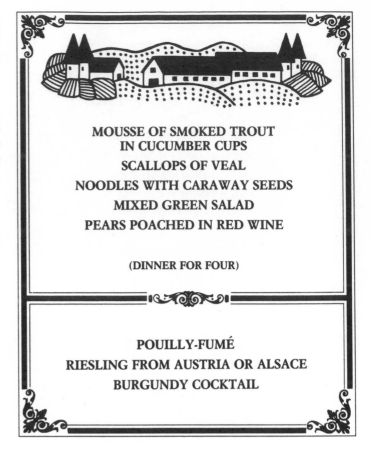

MOUSSE OF SMOKED TROUT
IN CUCUMBER CUPS
SCALLOPS OF VEAL
NOODLES WITH CARAWAY SEEDS
MIXED GREEN SALAD
PEARS POACHED IN RED WINE

(DINNER FOR FOUR)

POUILLY-FUMÉ
RIESLING FROM AUSTRIA OR ALSACE
BURGUNDY COCKTAIL

DINNER WITH AN AUSTRIAN FLAVOR

Though this dinner is simple to prepare, it is really designed for people who care about the subtleties of food. There are some quiet but complicated flavors here that will be appreciated by guests who know how to savor them.

You'll like the way the crispness of the Pouilly-Fumé works with the slightly smoky flavor of the first course. Riesling has a trace of fruit that sets off both the buttery veal and the pungency of caraway. The cocktail at the end is certainly different, and the currant flavor of the cassis in it is a knockout with the pears.

The menu is fresh and delicate. Resign yourself to cooking the veal and the noodles "to order"— surely not difficult, as you are serving only four. (It is a maxim that thin veal scallops are best cooked for no more than four at a time.) Use mild lettuces for the salad, with a gentle vinaigrette and minced fresh herbs, quite perfectly alone as a separate course and without wine. Then proceed to the made-ahead, wine-happy dessert.

MOUSSE OF SMOKED TROUT IN CUCUMBER CUPS

2 smoked trout, skinned and boned
1 1/4 cups heavy cream, in all
1 1/2 tablespoons bottled horseradish
3 drops Tabasco sauce
1/2 teaspoon lemon juice
2 seedless English cucumbers, peeled
Capers, in vinegar, drained

In a food processor, purée together the trout with 1/4 cup of the heavy cream, the horseradish, Tabasco sauce, and lemon juice. Press the mixture through a fine sieve into a bowl. Whip the remaining cup of cream and fold it into the trout purée.

Cut the cucumbers into pieces 3 inches long. Hollow out the centers, leaving a 1/2-inch seal at the bottom of each piece. Using a pastry bag, fill the cucumber cups with the mousse. Decorate with capers and serve with thinly sliced black bread.

Note: If the English cucumbers are very slim, instead of peeling them altogether, use a vegetable scraper to remove strips of the skin at 1/4-inch intervals for a pretty striped effect. Ordinary cucumbers are fine for this recipe, but their bitter waxed skins must be removed.

SCALLOPS OF VEAL

8 veal scallopini, pounded thin
Flour for dredging
1/4 pound unsalted butter, approximately
1/4 cup olive oil, approximately
2 tablespoons lemon juice
Peel of 1 lemon, cut into fine julienne strips
Freshly ground white pepper to taste

Dust the veal with the flour. In a large heavy skillet, heat half of both the butter and oil. Add 4 of the scallopini to the skillet and sauté until browned, about 1 1/2 minutes on each side. Remove each scallop to a hot platter as it is cooked. Repeat for the remaining 4 scallopini, replenishing the oil and butter as needed. Then add the lemon juice, lemon peel, and white pepper to the pan juices, bring to a simmer, stirring and scraping well, and pour over the veal.

NOODLES WITH CARAWAY SEEDS

1 pound fettuccine
4 tablespoons unsalted butter
1 tablespoon caraway seeds

Cook the pasta in boiling salted water until it is al dente. Drain and combine with the butter and caraway seeds.
Note: This is really best cooked just before serving.

PEARS POACHED IN RED WINE

3 cups red burgundy
1 large strip lemon peel
1 large strip orange peel
1/2 cup sugar
2 black peppercorns
4 firm ripe pears, peeled, cored, and halved
    lengthwise

Bring all the ingredients, except the pears, to a boil in a saucepan and simmer for 10 minutes. Poach the pears in the liquid until barely done, about 8 minutes. Remove from the heat and leave the pears in the liquid overnight in the refrigerator.

Drain and serve on individual plates accompanied by little cookies.

Note: This must be done at least 24 hours in advance to allow enough time for the pears to turn a rich winy color. The pears must be completely submerged; add more wine if necessary.

To cook 6 pears, poach them 3 at a time, adding a little more wine if necessary. Six pears are needed for the Wine Banquet dessert, page 78.

BURGUNDY COCKTAIL

For each drink:

4 ounces chilled red California burgundy
1/2 ounce *crème de cassis* liqueur

Pour the wine and liqueur over ice cubes in a wine glass when dessert is brought to the table.

ITALIAN DINNER

This is an informal meal designed for close friends, chilly evenings, and, especially, for people with hearty appetites—peasant food dressed up for company.

With these vegetables, you can't go wrong with Beaujolais—a Beaujolais nouveau if it's available. (It arrives, with an annual burst of publicity, in the month of November.) You need a big red wine for a stew as flavorful as this one. The sweet Moscato for the mousse may be either Californian or Italian.

Once the garlic vegetables, the stew, and the dessert are under control, conveniently ahead, put your attention to the rice. It is rich and wonderful and needs surveillance. The stew is generous; leftovers will reheat very nicely.

GARLIC VEGETABLES

2 cups olive oil
6 garlic cloves, sliced thin
1 teaspoon hot red pepper flakes
1 head cauliflower, separated into florets
24 baby carrots
24 button mushroom caps
2 unpeeled zucchini, cut into spears
1 1/2 tablespoons balsamic vinegar
3 tablespoons red wine vinegar
1/4 cup chopped fresh Italian parsley leaves
Salt to taste

Combine the oil, garlic, and hot pepper flakes in a jar. Let sit overnight.

Steam each vegetable separately until it is barely done. While they are still warm, dress them with the seasoned oil, adding also the vinegars and parsley. Cool and then taste for seasoning, adding salt to taste.

Serve at the table from a crock or tureen with a very crusty fresh bread.

VEAL STEW

8 pounds veal shoulder, cut into 1-inch cubes
3/4 cup all-purpose flour
1/2 cup olive oil
8 tablespoons unsalted butter, in all
1 large onion, chopped fine
4 cups chicken broth
One 35-ounce can plum tomatoes, drained and chopped
3 cups dry white wine
1 bunch Italian parsley, stems removed, chopped
2 tablespoons dried thyme
2 bay leaves
1 1/2 tablespoons *glace de viande* (available commercially)
1 cup tomato purée

Dust the veal with the flour. Heat the oil and 6 tablespoons of the butter in a heavy pot over high heat. Add the veal a few pieces at a time and brown the pieces on all sides. Remove to a platter as they are done. When all the veal is browned, return it to the pot.

Sauté the onion separately in the remaining 2 tablespoons of butter until transparent. Add it to the pot with the chicken broth, tomatoes, wine, parsley, thyme, and bay leaves. Bring to a boil, reduce the heat, cover partially, and simmer for 1 1/2 hours, or until the veal is tender. Add the meat glaze and tomato purée and simmer, uncovered, until the sauce is reduced and thickened, about 15 minutes. Serve from a casserole.

Note: This stew is best if made a day ahead and reheated.

SAFFRON RICE

1 teaspoon saffron threads
2 cups rice
1 small onion, minced
4 cups chicken broth
1/4 pound plus 2 tablespoons unsalted butter
5 tablespoons grated Parmesan cheese
Salt and freshly ground black pepper to taste

Dissolve the saffron in 1 tablespoon of the broth. Sauté the rice and onion in the 1/4 pound of butter until the onion is wilted. Add the remaining broth, bring to a boil and cover. When the liquid has been absorbed, about 15 minutes, uncover and add the remaining 2 tablespoons of butter and the Parmesan, saffron, and salt and pepper. Stir well.

Note: This should be made at the last minute; the butter and cheese form an emulsion that, when just made, produces a wonderful dish. If reheated, it has a tendency to separate.

RICOTTA MOUSSE

2 pounds ricotta
3/4 cup superfine sugar
2 tablespoons vanilla extract
2 tablespoons rum
1 teaspoon lemon juice
1 cup chopped candied fruit
2 eggs, separated

Press the ricotta through a sieve into a bowl and mix in the sugar, vanilla, rum, and lemon juice.

Beat the egg yolks until very pale in color and beat the whites until they form soft peaks. Fold the yolks into the cheese mixture first; then fold in the candied fruit and then the egg whites. Spoon into stemmed glasses and refrigerate. Serve chilled, with gaufrettes.

Notes: The mousse will hold in the refrigerator for about 3 hours. Gaufrettes are those old-fashioned thin, crisp, multilayered, fan-shaped cookies. They are charming with the mousse and available at specialty stores. If unavailable, substitute a cookie that has crunch and a mild flavor.

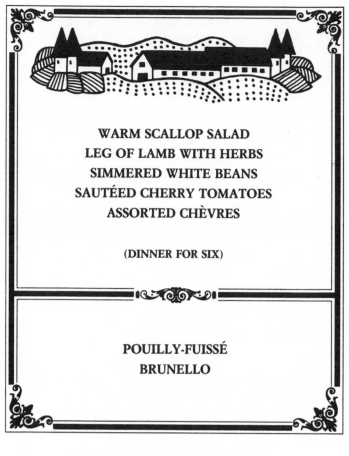

WARM SCALLOP SALAD
LEG OF LAMB WITH HERBS
SIMMERED WHITE BEANS
SAUTÉED CHERRY TOMATOES
ASSORTED CHÈVRES

(DINNER FOR SIX)

POUILLY-FUISSÉ
BRUNELLO

WINTER DINNER

New styles in food can often work to best advantage when combined with familiar traditional cooking. This menu lets you contrast a newly fashionable warm composed salad and goat cheeses with an absolutely simple leg of lamb—one of the great natural partners for wine.

The quality that makes Pouilly-Fuissé right for these scallops is its gentle softness. The lamb does well with a red wine that is moderately hearty and flavorful. The Brunello also does well with the cheeses. You could substitute a young, creamy Gorgonzola for the chèvres.

The roast goes into the oven about 1 hour and 15 minutes before it is carved. If you start the very quick-cooking scallops 30 minutes before carving the lamb, your timing should be about right.

WARM SCALLOP SALAD

1 head radicchio
1 head Bibb lettuce
1 bunch arugula
4 tablespoons unsalted butter
1 1/2 cups clam juice
1/2 cup dry vermouth
1 teaspoon Pernod
1 tablespoon pink peppercorns
1/2 teaspoon salt
1 pound sea scallops
Fresh chives cut into 1-inch lengths

Arrange the lettuces on individual plates, displaying the various colors.

Place all the remaining ingredients, except the scallops and chives, in a pan and cook over high heat for 3 to 5 minutes to reduce slightly. Add the scallops and cook until barely heated through. (This yields scallops that look and taste completely cooked, while at the same time preserving their texture and natural juices.) Taste for seasoning, also adding more Pernod if desired.

Place equal portions of the scallops on top of the lettuces, sprinkle with chives, and dress with the hot cooking liquid.

LEG OF LAMB WITH HERBS

1 cup olive oil
4 tablespoons dried rosemary
3 tablespoons dried basil
1 tablespoon dried tarragon
Freshly ground black pepper to taste
A whole leg of lamb

Preheat the oven to 425 degrees. Remove the fell and most of the fat from the lamb. Crush the oil and herbs together to make a paste and spread it over the meat. Roast to an internal temperature of 135 degrees, about 1 hour, or 10 minutes per pound, for rare. Let rest for at least 15 minutes before carving.

Note: The lamb should be carved in the dining room and the slices placed directly onto warmed dinner plates.

SIMMERED WHITE BEANS

Four 19-ounce cans white *cannellini* beans
4 tablespoons unsalted butter
1/4 cup finely chopped fresh parsley
Freshly ground black pepper to taste

Drain the beans, reserving about 3/4 cup of their liquid, rinse briefly in a sieve under cool running water, and allow to drain well again. Melt the butter in a casserole, add the beans and the reserved liquid, mix gently, and set aside.

Just before serving, heat beans to a simmer (do not allow them to cook), stir in the parsley, and season with pepper. After you carve the roast, spoon its juices over the beans as you serve them.

SAUTEED CHERRY TOMATOES

6 tablespoons unsalted butter
4 pint boxes cherry tomatoes, hulled
1 tablespoon sugar
Coarse salt and freshly ground black pepper to taste

In a large skillet, sauté the tomatoes in the melted butter, with the sugar, until just heated through. Sprinkle with salt and pepper. (Expect some of the skins to break.)

STUFFED MUSHROOMS
FISH CHOWDER
BERRY SHORTCAKE

(SUPPER FOR TWELVE)

DRY CHENIN BLANC
SWEET CHENIN BLANC

WINTER WEEKEND SUPPER

For guests who come to winter-beach country for a weekend out of doors, this menu is a warm and hearty welcome home. Neighbors are invited, too—it's dinner for a crowd. The chowder is like none you've ever tasted, velvety and packed with flavor, and the shortcake is sinful.

Though an Italian white wine would be a natural choice for the first course, the Chenin Blanc is a refreshing change. Switch to the sweet version, from California, or to a French Vouvray, for dessert.

The chowder is a project that allows country-weekend hosts to beg off from accompanying city guests on those arduous walks out into the cold and stay warm at home in the kitchen. It can best be shopped for in a seaside town, or, contradictorily, in a big city where it would work very well for a Saturday night supper. All the chowder preparation is done well ahead of the dinner hour. So, also, for the mushrooms. If the fresh berries for the dessert are too outrageously expensive, substitute Apple Crumble with Heavy Cream (see Recipe Index).

STUFFED MUSHROOMS

3 dozen large white mushrooms, stems removed
1/2 pound unsalted butter
1/2 cup white wine
1 bunch fresh Italian parsley leaves, chopped fine
1/4 pound prosciutto, cut into julienne strips
2 tablespoon dried basil
2 tablespoon dried tarragon
1 teaspoon dried oregano
1 teaspoon freshly ground black pepper
2 cups dry bread crumbs

Preheat the oven to 350 degrees.

Wash the mushrooms and dry thoroughly. Put 1 teaspoon of butter in each cap. Pour the wine into a large baking pan and set the mushrooms in the pan, cap side down, so the butter is on top. Bake until slightly softened, about 15 minutes. Remove the mushrooms, reserving the pan and its juices.

Place the remaining ingredients in the pan, stirring in the bread crumbs a bit at a time until you have a moist stuffing. (You will use anywhere from 1 cup to 2 cups of bread crumbs, depending on the amount of mushroom juice produced.) Taste for seasoning. Generously fill each mushroom cap with the stuffing. Place them on a baking sheet, stuffed side up.

To serve, reheat in a 375-degree oven until just heated through, but no longer.

FISH CHOWDER

4 quarts clam juice
2 bunches parsley sprigs
1 large onion, coarsely chopped
12 black peppercorns
Bones, scraps, and trimmings from the codfish
   (below)
6 large boiling potatoes, peeled
3 pounds mussels
3 dozen clams
1/2 cup brandy
1/2 cup dry vermouth
2 pounds medium-size shrimp, shelled and deveined
2 pounds sea scallops
3 pounds cod fillets
4 cups milk
4 cups heavy cream
1 teaspoon lemon juice
9 drops Tabasco sauce

In a large pot, bring the clam juice, parsley sprigs, onion, peppercorns, and fish bones and scraps to a boil. Simmer for 20 minutes. Strain into a clean pot.

Steam the potatoes until they can be easily pierced. Remove from the steamer, cut into bite-size pieces, and reserve.

Clean the mussels and clams. Place them in a heavy pan with the brandy and vermouth. Cover and cook over high heat until they just open, removing each one as soon as it does open. Discard the shells, reserving all the juices; pour these and the juices in the pot into the clam broth mixture. Reserve the clams and mussels.

Bring the broth to a boil and poach the shrimp and scallops for 1 minute; remove. Poach the cod fillets for 2 minutes and remove. Cut the shrimp and scallops in half and the cod into bite-size pieces. Reserve.

Add the cooked potatoes and the milk and cream to the broth; stir well to blend. Add the lemon juice and Tabasco sauce and taste for seasoning. When the soup has cooled completely, add all the seafood to the pot.

To serve, reheat the chowder gently until it is piping hot.

Note: The finished chowder will hold in the refrigerator if it must for up to 24 hours; it is not advisable to hold it any longer. Cover loosely with foil, not with a close-fitting lid.

BERRY SHORTCAKE

BERRY SAUCE
2 pint baskets strawberries
1/4 cup sugar
1 teaspoon lemon juice
1 pint basket blueberries
2 pint baskets raspberries

Hull and coarsely purée the strawberries. Add the sugar and lemon juice. Mix well. Add the blueberries and raspberries to the purée, cover, and marinate in the refrigerator for at least 1 hour. (The mixture will hold overnight.)

SHORTCAKE
4 cups all-purpose flour
2 tablespoons baking powder
1/2 teaspoon salt
4 cups heavy cream
2 tablespoons sugar
4 tablespoons unsalted butter
4 cups whipping cream, freshly whipped

Combine all the dry ingredients in a mixing bowl. Pour in the cream a little at a time to make a soft but not sticky dough. Knead the dough lightly on a flat surface and pat down to 1 1/2 inches thick. Use a cutter with a 2 1/2- or 3-inch diameter to cut out the dough. Put the scraps together and repeat the process until all the dough is used and you have at least 12 biscuits.

Melt the butter and dip both sides of each biscuit into it. Reserve the extra butter. Divide the biscuits between two heavy baking sheets and let rest for at least 1 hour at room temperature. Bake in a 450-degree oven until golden brown, about 15 minutes, turning them over once during baking.

Split the biscuits in half horizontally while they are still hot. Then put them on individual serving plates and drizzle the remaining melted butter on the bottom halves. Spoon on the berry mixture, cover with the top halves and then cover with whipped cream. Serve while still hot.

Notes: Put the biscuits in the oven to bake when your guests have finished the chowder. Do not despair if the whipped cream slips off the tops; it doesn't matter. Leftover biscuits are terrific toasted.

Almaden
CHENIN BLANC
OF CALIFORNIA

VINTED AND BOTTLED BY ALMADEN VINEYARDS
SAN JOSE, CA ALCOHOL 12%
BY VOLUME

EGGS WITH LETTUCES AND ASPARAGUS
POACHED TONGUE WITH RAISIN SAUCE
NEW POTATOES
APPLES BAKED IN WINE

(DINNER FOR SIX)

A RICH JOHANNISBERG RIESLING

INFORMAL DINNER

There is a moral to this menu: Simple, everyday ingredients can be given complex flavors. It isn't what you use, it's how you use it. And the tongue is an example of "cooking with wine" that is not in the least technical.

This menu, with an overtone of Central Europe, is a natural for the delicate and fruity sweetness of German-style wines. For a change, one wine can serve for all three courses, and you could choose an Auslese.

To poach the tongue, choose an inexpensive red wine, but not a harsh one. Tongue isn't served too often to guests, and it always seems to come as a pleasant surprise how delicious it is. There is no doubt, though, that most people would prefer not to look at the whole object, so slice it in the kitchen.

EGGS WITH LETTUCES AND ASPARAGUS

DRESSING
1/4 cup chopped *cornichons*
1 1/2 cups mayonnaise
1 to 2 tablespoons ketchup, for color and a little sweetness
2 tablespoons drained capers
1 tablespoon chopped fresh tarragon, or to taste
1 tablespoon chopped fresh Italian parsley leaves, or to taste
Freshly ground black pepper to taste

Combine all the ingredients in a bowl and taste for seasoning. The sauce should be pale pink.

THE SALAD
12 asparagus stalks
6 hard-boiled eggs
Assorted lettuces (Boston, Bibb, endive, watercress)

Snap off the asparagus stems and reserve for a soup. Trim the tips to even lengths and blanch them in boiling water until crisp-tender. Peel the eggs and cut them in half. Line individual plates with the assorted greens. Place 2 eggs halves on top and spoon the dressing over them, masking them completely. Garnish with the asparagus tips.

POACHED TONGUE WITH RAISIN SAUCE

TONGUE

One 3-to 4-pound smoked beef tongue
1 bottle red wine
12 black peppercorns
2 bay leaves
1 small onion, quartered

Put the tongue in a pot, pour in the wine, and add water to just cover it. Add the remaining ingredients, bring to a boil, and remove any scum that rises to the surface. Reduce the heat to a low simmer and cook until tender, about 3 hours (when the little bones at the back of the tongue can be moved easily). Remove the tongue from the poaching liquid and drain.

When the tongue is cool, cut off the fat from the root, remove the little bones, and peel off the skin. Return the tongue to the pot and let it sit in the liquid. Reheat in the liquid to serve.

To serve, slice thinly on the diagonal and arrange in overlapping slices on a platter.

Note: Reserve the cooking liquid. Later, boil it down and freeze it. Use with stock and more wine when cooking another tongue or a ham.

RAISIN SAUCE
One 1-pound box golden raisins
3 cups sweet Riesling-type wine
1 cup chicken broth
1 teaspoon lemon juice, or to taste

Combine the raisins, wine, and broth in a saucepan and boil until the raisins are completely tender. Reserve 1 cup of the mixture. Coarsely purée the rest and push this through a sieve. Add the reserved portion of raisins and season with lemon juice. Serve warm.

NEW POTATOES

12 small new potatoes
4 tablespoons unsalted butter

Wash and peel the potatoes. Steam or boil them until they are tender. Melt the butter in a saucepan. Remove from the heat, add the potatoes, and toss until they are coated. Cover and let sit. Reheat to serve.

APPLES BAKED IN WINE

6 large baking apples, such as Rome Beauty
1 cup white wine
Peel of 1 lemon
Peel of 1 orange
1 cup dark brown sugar
2 tablespoons ground ginger
6 tablespoons unsalted butter
2 cups heavy cream

Preheat the oven to 350 degrees. Peel and core the apples. Place them in a baking pan, pour in the wine, and add the lemon and orange peels. Combine the sugar and ginger in a small bowl. Place an equal amount of the mixture in each apple and put a large pat of butter on the top.

Bake until the apples are tender but still holding their shape, about 40 minutes. Baste with the pan juices occasionally.

Serve at room temperature and pass the cream separately.

FRIED MOZZARELLA WITH ANCHOVY SAUCE
CHICKEN CONTADINA
CHOPPED TOMATO AND RED ONION SALAD
MARINATED FRUIT

(DINNER FOR SIX)

SOAVE OR CALIFORNIA CHABLIS
CHIANTI
MUSCATO OR ASTI SPUMANTE

CASUAL SUNDAY DINNER

This Sunday dinner is for those who love the simplicity and gutsy flavors of rustic Italian cooking. The mood should be informal; use pottery plates and stemless glasses for the wine.

For the first two courses, ask your guests the classic Italian waiters' wine query: "You want red or you want white?" Either one does well with the anchovy sauce or the chicken. Refined wines would be out of place and uncomfortable at this meal.

The chicken will be made at least a day ahead and reheated; the salad and the fruit await in the refrigerator. So the mozzarella for the first course is your one job after guests arrive.

FRIED MOZZARELLA WITH ANCHOVY SAUCE

ANCHOVY SAUCE
1/2 cup olive oil
2 cans flat anchovies in oil
3 tablespoons chopped Italian parsley leaves
1/2 tablespoon lemon juice

Combine all the ingredients, including the anchovy oil, and purée with a mortar and pestle or in a small bowl with a wooden spoon.

FRIED MOZZARELLA
Two 1-pound packages mozzarella
1/2 cup all-purpose flour
2 eggs, beaten
2 cups dry bread crumbs
1 cup olive oil
6 lemon slices
Fresh Italian parsley leaves for garnish

Slice each mozzarella lengthwise into three equal pieces. Dip first into the flour and then into the eggs and then into the bread crumbs. Leave on a baking sheet, uncovered, until dry, at least 1 hour, turning once.

Preheat the oven to 375 degrees. Heat the olive oil in a frying pan until it is hot but not smoking. Fry two pieces of mozzarella at a time until golden brown on each side. Drain and keep warm in the oven while you fry the rest.

To serve, place mozzarella in the center of a plate and spoon on 1 or 2 teaspoons of the anchovy sauce. Top with a slice of lemon and garnish with a few leaves of Italian parsley. Pass the remainder of the sauce at the table.

CHICKEN CONTADINA

Two 2 1/2- to 3-pound chickens and their livers
1/2 to 1 cup olive oil
2 heads garlic, peeled
2 large onions, chopped
9 medium-size boiling potatoes, peeled and quartered
1 cup Italian parsley leaves, coarsely chopped
1 teaspoon hot red pepper flakes
Two 10-ounce packages frozen artichoke hearts, defrosted and cut in half
1 cup chicken broth
1 teaspoon lemon juice
Salt, freshly ground black pepper, and Tabasco sauce to taste

Have your butcher cut up the chicken as he would for frying. Using a cleaver and wood mallet, further cut the chicken into 2-inch pieces, discarding any unrewarding bony pieces. Chop the chicken livers coarsely and reserve. Coat the bottom of a heavy pot with some of the oil. Sauté the chicken until it starts to brown. Add the garlic and remove from the heat.

In another pan, sauté the onion in a little oil until it is transparent; then add the onion to the chicken. In the onion pan, sauté the potatoes for about 5 minutes, adding additional oil if necessary. Add the potatoes to the chicken along with the parsley and hot pepper flakes. Cover and cook over low heat for 40 minutes, stirring occasionally. Then add the artichoke hearts and chopped livers to the pot. Continue to cook for 10 minutes. Add chicken broth, lemon juice, and salt, pepper, and Tabasco sauce. Bring to a good simmer and serve hot.

Notes: This recipe provides an opportunity to use *all* the chicken or any chicken parts you may have on hand. Small pieces are appropriate. The recipe is flexible. You can add Italian sausages (hot or sweet), mushrooms, and the minced giblets. If adding sausages, boil them separately until their color has changed, cut them into large chunks, and add them to the pot for the last 20 minutes of cooking time.

Chicken Contadina does not freeze well, but it will hold beautifully in the refrigerator for up to three days. So make this dish ahead, cover, refrigerate, and remove the congealed fat before reheating.

CHOPPED TOMATO AND RED ONION SALAD

1 cup olive oil
3 tablespoons sherry vinegar
1 tablespoon lemon juice
1 teaspoon sugar
1/2 teaspoon salt
3 drops Tabasco sauce
Freshly ground black pepper to taste
1 1/2 red onions, coarsely chopped
6 to 8 tomatoes, cut into bite-size chunks
1/4 cup chopped fresh Italian parsley leaves

Combine the oil, vinegar, and seasonings. Marinate the onions and tomatoes in the vinaigrette for at least 2 hours. Taste for seasoning, adding more lemon juice if needed. Serve on individual plates and sprinkle with the chopped parsley.

Note: If the tomatoes are thick skinned, it's best to peel them.

MARINATED FRUIT

1 cup white wine
2 tablespoons orange liqueur
Zest and juice of 1 orange
1/4 cup sugar, or to taste
8 to 10 cups berries and assorted cut-up fresh fruit

Combine the liquids and sugar in a large bowl. Add the fruit and marinate for at least 2 hours. Serve with little Italian cookies.

Note: Use either dry or sweet wine; if sweet, adjust the amount of sugar to taste.

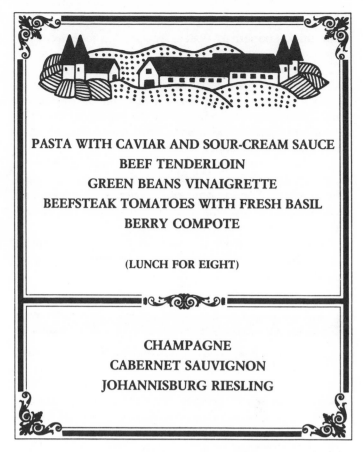

PASTA WITH CAVIAR AND SOUR-CREAM SAUCE
BEEF TENDERLOIN
GREEN BEANS VINAIGRETTE
BEEFSTEAK TOMATOES WITH FRESH BASIL
BERRY COMPOTE

(LUNCH FOR EIGHT)

CHAMPAGNE
CABERNET SAUVIGNON
JOHANNISBURG RIESLING

SUMMER LUXURY

Expensive ingredients are like jewelry; if you use them, show them off. Using them simply does it best. This menu relies on fresh produce, a controlled extravagance of butter and cream, and, for each dish, a careful but not elaborate presentation. A touch of luxury in the wines is recommended, too.

Of course, Champagne with caviar. What else? The Cabernet does justice to the beef and also flatters the summer vegetables. And the refreshing, fruity coolness of Riesling is just right for the berries.

To achieve its full effect, this menu is planned so it can be set out on a sideboard and served plate by plate. This includes the pasta, which arrives first in a warmed dish to be served and sauced in small portions, not to rob the tenderloin of the spotlight.

PASTA WITH CAVIAR AND SOUR-CREAM SAUCE

4 cups heavy cream
1/4 pound unsalted butter
1 cup sour cream
10 drops Tabasco sauce
1 teaspoon lemon juice
Freshly ground black pepper to taste
2 pounds imported corkscrew pasta
3/4 pound domestic golden whitefish caviar
1/4 cup chopped fresh chives

Put the heavy cream and butter in a saucepan and boil until thick enough to coat a spoon. Remove from the heat.

Put the sour cream in a bowl. Whisking continuously, add the heavy cream mixture to the sour cream, 1 tablespoon at a time, so the two creams will be thoroughly combined. Return this mixture to the saucepan. To serve, reheat until warm and season with the Tabasco sauce, lemon juice, and pepper.

Just before serving, cook the pasta until al dente in salted water and drain. Divide the pasta equally among 8 heated plates. Spoon some sauce over each serving and garnish each on top with 2 generous tablespoons of caviar. Dust with the chopped chives.

Note: Golden caviar can be frozen. It is not expensive and its crunchy texture makes it particularly appealing for this dish.

BEEF TENDERLOIN

One whole beef tenderloin weighing 9 to 10 pounds before trimming

Ask your butcher to prepare the tenderloin for roasting. It may be barded with fat and tied. Or you can merely rub it generously with olive oil.

Preheat the oven to 425 degrees. Place the beef in a roasting pan and roast for 45 minutes to 1 hour, or until it reaches an internal temperature of 120 degrees for rare. Remove from the oven and let rest. (Remove the strings and barding fat.) Carve into slices 1/2 inch thick only when ready to serve.

GREEN BEANS VINAIGRETTE

1 1/2 pounds green beans, with ends trimmed
8 black peppercorns
1 cup olive oil
1/4 cup red wine vinegar
1/8 teaspoon dry mustard
1/2 teaspoon salt
1 teaspoon balsamic vinegar
Freshly ground black pepper to taste
3 pinches cayenne pepper
1 small onion, thinly sliced

Boil the beans in salted water, along with peppercorns, until crisp but tender. Immediately drain and put in cold water to set the color. Drain again and set aside.

Combine the remaining ingredients, except for the onion, in a small bowl and whisk until blended. Toss this vinaigrette with the green beans in a bowl, along with the onion, cover, and marinate in the refrigerator overnight. Taste for seasoning.

Serve from an elegant bowl, using a slotted spoon.

BEEFSTEAK TOMATOES WITH FRESH BASIL

4 large ripe beefsteak tomatoes
Salt and freshly ground black pepper to taste
1 teaspoon sugar
Fresh basil leaves

Core and slice the tomatoes; then sprinkle them with salt and pepper, and sugar and set aside on a plate. Serve cool, but not cold. There may be some weeping from the tomatoes, so transfer them to a platter not too long before serving. Decorate generously with small, perfect basil leaves.

BERRY COMPOTE

1 medium-size cantaloupe
2 pint baskets blueberries
1 pint basket strawberries, hulled
1 pint basket raspberries
1 cup orange juice
1 cup white wine
1/4 cup sugar
1/4 cup orange liqueur
Confectioner's sugar

Seed the cantaloupe and cut out the flesh with a mellon baller. In a large bowl, combine all the ingredients, except 1 pint of the blueberries and the confectioner's sugar. Toss, cover, and marinate in the refrigerator for several hours. Taste for sweetness.

To serve, place the marinated fruit in a glass bowl and cover with an all-blue layer of the reserved blueberries on top. Sprinkle with confectioner's sugar and decorate with one large perfect strawberry.

Note: This compote takes very kindly to a good dollop of whipped cream served from a sauceboat.

**CROSTINI
VEAL CHOPS WITH ROSEMARY
SAUTÉED ESCAROLE
STRAWBERRIES AND ZABAGLIONE SAUCE**

(LUNCH FOR SIX)

**BARDOLINO
CHIANTI CLASSICO
ASTI SPUMANTE**

ITALIAN SUNDAY LUNCH

Italian cooking, as just about everybody knows by now, has a broad range of flavors and styles to offer. This menu is simple, but it works the Italian theme up to an elegant finish.

Should you use only Italian wines with an Italian dinner or might you mix? Of course you can mix. This menu does work particularly well with wines from Italy, but it would be interesting to look for California counterparts—such as California rosé, light Zinfandel, and demi-sec Champagne.

Crostini are merely superlative toasted-cheese sandwiches and fun to make. They are broiled at the last minute, however, so if your broiler also heats your oven, lower the heat immediately when you take out the *crostini,* as the veal chops are finished in a 375-degree oven.

CROSTINI

**1 long loaf of crusty Italian-style bread, cut into 18
    slices 1 inch thick
1/2 to 1 cup olive oil
2 garlic cloves, sliced
One 35-ounce can plum tomatoes
1 1/2 pounds mozzarella, sliced thin
2 cans flat anchovies in oil
3 lemons, halved**

Sauté the bread on both sides in a 1/2 cup of the olive oil, with the garlic, until golden brown; add more oil if needed. Remove to a broiling pan. Drain the tomatoes and slice them into rounds.

When ready to serve, cover each piece of bread with a slice of mozzarella and top with tomato rounds. Crisscross with anchovies and drizzle with the anchovy oil. Broil the *crostini* under high heat until the cheese melts, about 2 minutes. Serve three *crostini* and half a lemon to each guest.

Note: In summer, fresh tomatoes, of course, are preferable if they are perfectly ripe, thin-skinned (or peeled), and don't have big pockets of seeds.

VEAL CHOPS WITH ROSEMARY

**6 veal chops, cut at least 1 1/2 inches thick
1/2 cup olive oil
2 tablespoons dried rosemary, crushed**

Preheat the oven to 375 degrees. Dip the chops in the oil and sprinkle heavily with the rosemary. First brown the veal for about 3 minutes on each side on top of the stove in a sauté pan. Transfer the chops to a broiler pan as they are browned. Then place the chops on the broiler pan in the oven, uncovered, and continue cooking, for about 10 minutes.

Note: This is an efficient way of controlling both the browning and the juiciness of the veal. You do not have to go on to the second stage immediately after the browning. Finish the cooking when most convenient. The chops are done when you poke them with a finger and the meat resists but still gives a little under the pressure.

SAUTEED ESCAROLE

**2 pounds escarole
1/2 cup olive oil
3 garlic cloves, sliced thin
Salt and freshly ground black pepper to taste**

Cut the escarole leaves into 4- or 5-inch lengths, rinse, and drain well. Heat the oil and garlic together in a large saucepan. Add the escarole, cover, and cook until the leaves are completely wilted, about 10 to 15 minutes. Stir occasionally. Sprinkle with salt and pepper and serve tepid.

Note: You will need a slotted spoon for serving. If you take care not to over-wilt the escarole, you can cook it ahead and reheat it gently when wanted.

STRAWBERRIES AND ZABAGLIONE SAUCE

**9 egg yolks
1/4 cup sugar
1/2 cup dry marsala
1/4 cup Grand Marnier
4 pint boxes strawberries, hulled**

Put the egg yolks, sugar, and liquors in the top of a double boiler over barely simmering water. Beat the mixture constantly with a whisk until it is very fluffy and has doubled in volume, about 10 to 12 minutes. Strain through a coarse sieve into a bowl, cover, and cool in the refrigerator.

Before serving, whisk the sauce. Arrange the strawberries on individual plates and spoon the sauce over them.

Notes: Heat the egg mixture very slowly to avoid curdling. The sieving is to eliminate any bits of coagulated egg that might have formed. When chilled, *zabaglione* loses volume and turns into a thick custard sauce when rewhisked.

FOUR-ONION CUSTARD TART
ROAST CORNISH HENS
WILD RICE SALAD
SNOW PEAS
MARINATED ORANGE SLICES

(LUNCH FOR SIX)

CHENIN BLANC
GEWÜRZTRAMINER

AUTUMN FESTIVITIES

Not all fall weekends are for football. Now and then, who doesn't feel the need for something less informal? Here's a menu that is casual and, at the same time, an event.

No fancy bottles should intrude upon this informal lunch. An "off-dry" Chenin Blanc will be very compatible with the subtle sweetness of the cooked onions. (To begin, serve some of this wine as an apéritif.) The flavorful game hen and the rice salad need something with more character, however. Here the richness and unique spicy fragrance of a Gewürztraminer seem right.

Add up the time you expect to allot to apéritifs and then to serving the first course and the chances are you'll come up with about one hour—indicating that you want to put the game hens in the oven shortly before the last guest arrives. Everything else is already done except the snow peas, which you can steam when you go to the kitchen to give the birds their final basting. Sharp, rather small knives at each place setting are in order when serving small whole birds.

FOUR-ONION CUSTARD TART

2 cups heavy cream
1/2 cup grated Swiss cheese
1/2 teaspoon freshly ground white pepper
1/2 teaspoon cayenne pepper
3 eggs, lightly beaten
1/4 cup chopped onion
2 tablespoons chopped scallions
2 tablespoons unsalted butter, in all
Piecrust dough for 9-inch pan
1 small bunch leeks, white part only, cut into
    julienne strips
1 tablespoon chopped chives

Preheat the oven to 450 degrees.

Scald the cream and add the cheese and white and cayenne peppers. Stir well. Remove from the heat and stir in the eggs.

Sauté the onion and scallion in 1 tablespoon of the butter until they are translucent. Stir into the custard and set aside.

Line a 9-inch tart pan with your favorite short crust dough recipe. Cover the dough with aluminum foil and fill with dried beans or rice. Bake for 8 minutes, remove the foil and beans or rice, and bake for 6 minutes, or until light golden brown. Remove and reduce the oven temperature to 375 degrees.

Sauté the leeks in the remaining tablespoon of butter until wilted. Spread them on the bottom of the baked shell. Pour in the custard mixture. Bake until set, about 30 minutes. Sprinkle the top with the chives. Serve at room temperature.

ROAST CORNISH GAME HENS

8 tablespoons unsalted butter
2 tablespoons dried rosemary
6 Cornish game hens, fresh, not frozen

Preheat the oven to 375 degrees.

Make a paste of the butter and rosemary and rub it over the birds. Place the hens in a large roasting pan and roast them, uncovered, until browned and tender, about 45 minutes, basting every 15 minutes with the pan juices.

WILD RICE SALAD

VINAIGRETTE DRESSING
3 tablespoons sherry vinegar
1 cup olive oil
1 tablespoon balsamic vinegar
1/2 teaspoon lemon juice
6 drops Tabasco sauce
Freshly ground black pepper to taste

Combine all the ingredients in a bowl and set aside at room temperature.

WILD RICE
3 cups chicken broth
1 1/2 cups wild rice
1 teaspoon salt
3 celery stalks, chopped fine
1 small onion, chopped fine
1 green pepper, chopped fine
1 sweet red pepper, chopped fine
2 tablespoons unsalted butter
1/2 cup coarsely chopped pecans
One 8-ounce can water chestnuts, drained and
    chopped fine

Bring the chicken broth to a boil, stir in the rice, and add the salt. Boil until the rice is tender, about 30 minutes. Drain well.

Sauté the celery, onion, and peppers in the butter until just wilted. Combine with the rice. Add the pecans and water chestnuts. While the rice is still warm, toss the salad with the vinaigrette dressing. Taste for seasoning, adding more sherry vinegar if desired. Serve at room temperature.

SNOW PEAS

1 1/2 pounds snow peas
1 teaspoon lemon juice
Salt and freshly ground black pepper to taste

Steam the snow peas briefly, about 3 minutes, and season with the lemon juice and salt and pepper.

MARINATED ORANGE SLICES

6 navel oranges
1/4 cup sugar
Grated rind of 1 medium-size lemon
2 tablespoons lemon juice
2 cups orange juice

Peel the oranges, removing all the white pith and the thin skin beneath. Cut the oranges crosswise into slices approximately 3/8 inch thick and pick out any seeds. Put the slices in a shallow serving bowl and add the sugar, lemon rind, and lemon and orange juices. Cover the bowl and refrigerate for at least 4 hours, turning the slices a few times in the liquid. Serve with small cookies.

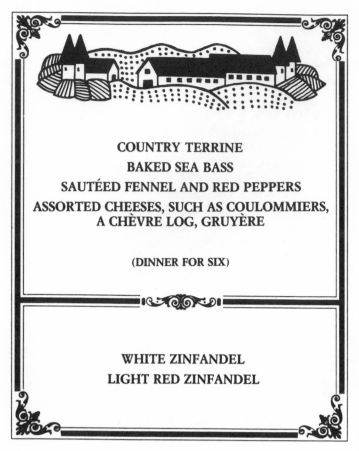

COUNTRY TERRINE

BAKED SEA BASS

SAUTÉED FENNEL AND RED PEPPERS

ASSORTED CHEESES, SUCH AS COULOMMIERS,
A CHÈVRE LOG, GRUYÈRE

(DINNER FOR SIX)

WHITE ZINFANDEL
LIGHT RED ZINFANDEL

SUPPER ON A SUMMER TERRACE

Simple French meals have something permanently appealing about them that cannot be upstaged. A pâté, a fresh fish, vegetables cooked with attention, good cheese, good bread—these are the components here, done for summertime with the flavors of the south of France. There, the fish would be the famous *loup,* the true European bass. Fresh figs might be added for dessert.

Appropriate to a summer's evening, the menu is light and not elaborate. But the food is bursting with assertive flavors. So while the weather suggests white wine, the food wants red. Choose a middle path, a white Zinfandel (a rosé would also be good) and then show off the versatility of the grape by pouring a slightly chilled light red Zinfandel with the cheeses. Ideally, it should be five or six years old.

1 pound fresh sausage meat
1/2 pound sliced boiled ham, cut into small dice
2 eggs
1 small onion, chopped and sautéed in butter
1 teaspoon dried tarragon
2 tablespoons chopped fresh parsley
1/4 cup brandy
1/4 teaspoon ground mace
1/2 teaspoon salt
Freshly ground black pepper to taste
1/4 pound unsalted butter, softened
1/2 pound bacon, sliced thin
1 pound cooked chicken, diced small
6 chicken livers, sautéed in butter

Combine the sausage meat, ham, eggs, onion, tarragon, parsley, brandy, mace, salt, pepper, and butter in a bowl. Preheat the oven to 350 degrees.

Line a 1 1/2-quart casserole with three quarters of the bacon. Top with a layer of the sausage mixture and then of chicken. Repeat until all ingredients are used. Finish with a layer of sausage; then press in the chicken livers down the center and cover with the remaining bacon. Cover the casserole, place in a pan of hot water, and bake for 2 hours. Chill for at least 4 hours before slicing. Serve with crusty French bread and *cornichons.*

BAKED SEA BASS

Two 3-pound sea bass, cleaned, head and tail on
1/2 teaspoon freshly ground black pepper
2 teaspoons lemon juice
4 slices bacon
1/4 pound unsalted butter
Lemon slices

Preheat the oven to 400 degrees.

Rub the inside of the fish with the pepper and lemon juice. In a large baking dish place each fish on its own piece of buttered aluminum foil. (This helps in handling the fish.) Crisscross the fish with the bacon and dot with butter.

Measure the thickness of the fish at its widest point and bake for 8 minutes per inch, basting at least three times during cooking. Remove from the oven, discard the bacon, and let the fish stand for 10 minutes. Remove the skin from both sides, transfer the fish to a platter, and decorate with the lemon slices.

SAUTEED FENNEL AND RED PEPPERS

6 sweet red peppers
6 tablespoons unsalted butter, in all
Freshly ground black pepper to taste
4 fennel bulbs, trimmed and cut into julienne strips
1/2 teaspoon anise-flavored liqueur

In a hot broiler, char the peppers on all sides. Place them in a brown paper bag for 4 minutes. Remove them from the bag and peel off the skins. (Note: the burnt peppers steam in the bag, which loosens their skins.) Quarter the peppers lengthwise, remove the pith and seeds, and set aside.

When the bass comes out of the oven, sauté the peppers in 3 tablespoons of the butter until heated through and season with black pepper. In another pan, sauté the fennel in the remaining butter, adding the liqueur, until tender but still crisp.

To serve, arrange the red peppers and fennel in a large gratin pan in concentric circles, with the fennel on the outside.

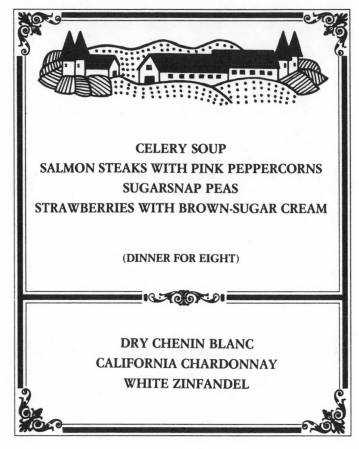

CELERY SOUP
SALMON STEAKS WITH PINK PEPPERCORNS
SUGARSNAP PEAS
STRAWBERRIES WITH BROWN-SUGAR CREAM

(DINNER FOR EIGHT)

DRY CHENIN BLANC
CALIFORNIA CHARDONNAY
WHITE ZINFANDEL

SIMPLE DINNER WITH ELEGANT WINES

The progression of flavors is one key to menu planning, and a progression of colors can be another. Here's a dinner that begins with the celadon green of the soup, followed by the rosy brown of the salmon and peas of brilliant green. It closes with scarlet berries and a creamy pale tan sauce.

Here's an opportunity to explore several white wines all from California. Their variety not only complements the food, they also show off what vintners here at home are doing.

This very simple menu can be made almost at a moment's notice (the soup can certainly be made ahead, however), and it can easily be reduced to serve as few as you wish. The last-minute cooking works easily to serve up to eight; more than that would depend on the size of your broiler.

CELERY SOUP

2 quarts roughly chopped celery
4 tablespoons unsalted butter
3 quarts chicken broth
6 black peppercorns
1 bunch fresh Italian parsley leaves, chopped
1 cup rice
1 cup heavy cream
1 teaspoon lemon juice
Freshly ground white pepper to taste
2 celery stalks, diced small

Put the chopped celery, butter, chicken broth, peppercorns, parsley, and rice, in a heavy pot and cook until mushy, about 25 minutes. Purée in a food processor and add the cream, lemon juice, and pepper. Strain through a fine sieve. Reheat and serve from a tureen. Pass the diced celery to spoon onto the soup.

SALMON STEAKS WITH PINK PEPPERCORNS

8 salmon steaks cut 1 inch thick
Generous amount of pink peppercorns

Preheat a broiling pan. Scatter the peppercorns over the salmon, pressing them down slightly into the flesh. Place the steaks on the hot broiling pan and broil close to the flame until the salmon is done and the peppercorns are slightly scorched, about 2 to 3 minutes. Do not turn.

Note: People probably won't believe the salmon will be done so quickly, so just don't tell them about it until later. It works.

SUGARSNAP PEAS

1 1/2 pounds sugarsnap peas, ends trimmed
4 tablespoons unsalted butter
1 teaspoon sugar
Salt and freshly ground black pepper to taste
1 teaspoon lemon juice

Cook the peas in boiling water for 1 minute; then drain. Toss with the butter and add the seasonings.

STRAWBERRIES WITH BROWN-SUGAR CREAM

4 cups sour cream
1 1/2 cups light brown sugar, approximately
1/2 teaspoon vanilla extract
4 pint baskets large strawberries, hulled

Combine the sour cream, sugar, and vanilla. Arrange the strawberries on individual plates and pass the sauce separately.

Note: The color of the sauce should be café-au-lait. Change the proportion of sour cream and sugar to taste.

PIMIENTOS AND ANCHOVIES
CHICKEN BREAST MILANESE
ZUCCHINI STRIPS WITH PINE NUTS
POACHED PEARS WITH MERINGUE
RASPBERRY SAUCE

(DINNER FOR FOUR)

VERDICCHIO
DOLCETTO
LATE HARVEST SAUVIGNON

FESTIVE SATURDAY NIGHT

What makes this menu festive are its colors—reds, greens, golden browns—and the fact that it is designed just for four, for one's closest friends. The baked dessert is particularly beautiful.

There is a time for simple table wines, and this is one of them. In keeping with the Italian theme, first, the clear, refreshing, light Verdicchio. Then, a chilled Dolcetto—proof that red wines go with chicken (a Beaujolais would also work well). For dessert, a shift to elegance with a sweet dessert wine; or, if you'd like to end with bubbles, any sparkling wine that is not Brut.

The key to cooking this attractive dinner is finishing the advance preparation and having everything lined up ready to go for the final cooking—the chicken, the zucchini and pine nuts, the pears and raspberry sauce. The first course is finished in advance. Use an electric beater to whip the meringue for the dessert shortly before you are ready to bake it. Because you are serving only four, timing will not be a problem. The recipes could easily be multiplied to serve more, but over all the menu might then prove inconvenient.

PIMIENTOS AND ANCHOVIES

4 large sweet red peppers
1 cup olive oil
1/4 cup red wine vinegar
1 can anchovies fillets in oil, drained
Freshly ground black pepper to taste

In a hot broiler, char the peppers on all sides. Remove them and place them in a brown paper bag for 4 minutes. Remove from the bag and peel off the skins. (Note: The peppers steam in the paper bag, which loosens their skins.) Cut each pepper into quarters lengthwise and remove the pith and seeds. Put in a container with the olive oil and vinegar to marinate for several hours or overnight.

To serve, place 4 pieces of pepper on each plate and crisscross with the anchovies. Pass extra vinegar and a pepper mill.

CHICKEN BREAST MILANESE

8 chicken breast cutlets
4 eggs
2 tablespoon water
2 cups dry bread crumbs
1 cup grated Parmesan cheese
1 cup all-purpose flour
Olive oil for frying
2 lemons, cut into wedges

Lightly pound the cutlets between sheets of wax paper until flat and even. Combine the eggs and water and beat lightly. Mix the bread crumbs and cheese together. Dredge the cutlets with the flour, shaking off any excess. Then dip them into the egg and water mixture and then into the bread crumbs and cheese mixture. The cutlets should be well coated. Let sit on a baking sheet, uncovered, at room temperature until the coating is partially dry, about 1 hour. Turn once.

Pour olive oil into a heavy skillet to a depth of 1/4 inch. Heat the oil until it is hot, but not smoking. Fry the cutlets two at a time, turning once. Wait until a golden brown crust forms on the bottom before turning. Add more oil to the pan as needed. Don't rush. If a crust hasn't completely formed, the cutlets will stick. (They will still taste fine; just serve pretty side up.) Reserve in a warm oven until all are fried. Serve with lemon wedges.

Note: This looks very pretty if you serve the cutlets all together on a large heated platter surrounded by the lemon wedges. If there are leftovers, the cutlets are delicious cold.

ZUCCHINI STRIPS WITH PINE NUTS

1 cup pine nuts
1/2 cup olive oil, in all
8 zucchini, scrubbed but not peeled
2 tablespoons dry vermouth
1 teaspoon lemon juice
1/4 teaspoon salt
Freshly ground black pepper to taste

Sauté the pine nuts in 1/4 cup of the olive oil until golden. Drain well on paper towels and reserve.

Cut the zucchini lengthwise into long, thin strips so it looks like green spaghetti. Discard most of the inside white part. Cover the zucchini and set aside.

When you are ready to serve, coat the bottom of a heavy skillet with olive oil. Set over high heat and put in the zucchini strips. Add the remaining ingredients. Stir constantly until the zucchini just starts to wilt, 2 to 3 minutes. Immediately remove from the heat. Toss in the pine nuts, mix, and serve.

Notes: A good tool for cutting the zucchini is a lemon stripper or a slightly larger version of the same tool intended for vegetables. The zucchini cannot be reheated without getting soggy.

POACHED PEARS WITH MERINGUE

POACHED PEARS WITH MERINGUE
2 cups water
1 cup granulated sugar, in all
1 cup dry vermouth
1 halved vanilla bean
2 firm ripe pears, peeled, halved, and cored
1 sheet parchment paper

5 egg whites
3/4 cup slivered almonds
3/4 cup confectioner's sugar

Combine the water, 2/3 cup of the granulated sugar, vermouth, and vanilla bean in a pan large enough to hold the pear halves in a single layer. Boil for 3 minutes.

Place the pears in the hot syrup, flat side down. Cover with parchment paper; this keeps the pears submerged in the syrup and prevents discoloring. Over low heat, poach gently until the pears are partially cooked yet still firm, about 3 minutes. Remove from the heat. Reserve the pears in the syrup, still covered with the parchment paper.

Preheat the broiler.

In a bowl, first whip the egg whites to a froth. Then, still beating, gradually add the remaining 1/3 cup of granulated sugar until the whites are glossy and thick.

Drain the pears and pat them dry. Lay them flat side down in a shallow ovenproof dish. Using a pastry bag, or a spatula, completely cover each pear half liberally with the meringue. Stand the almond slivers on top, so the pears look like white porcupines. Sprinkle heavily with confectioner's sugar. Broil until the meringue is glazed and lightly browned and the nuts are just slightly burnt, about 3 minutes.

RASPBERRY SAUCE

One 10-ounce package frozen raspberries
2 tablespoons raspberry liqueur
1/2 teaspoon lemon juice
Sugar to taste

Thaw the berries; then press them through a sieve into a bowl. Add the remaining ingredients.

To serve, place each pear half on a plate with an attractive border and surround with the raspberry sauce.

Note: This dessert doesn't hold well ahead, because the meringue starts to weep. But you can poach the pears up to a day in advance. The raspberry sauce can be held up to 2 days.

OYSTERS IN RAMEKINS
SAUTÉED WILD MUSHROOMS
AND FETTUCCINE
MIXED GREEN SALAD
APPLE GALETTE

(DINNER FOR EIGHT)

MUSCADET
CALIFORNIA CABERNET
CHAMPAGNE

FALL FANTASY

Wild mushrooms are, at once, among the homeliest and most delicious things on earth. Their flavors are complex and rich beyond description. Whenever they appear, they are the star attraction.

Muscadet, crisp as a fall day, tart and refreshing, is produced near the sea and has a special affinity for shellfish. Similarly, an earthy Cabernet with a bouquet that makes you think of truffles or fine tobacco is a natural companion for a dish filled with the musky flavor of wild mushrooms. Then stage a bubbly finish by serving a not-too-dry champagne from California or a sparkling wine from the Loire Valley.

There is no doubt in this menu that the cook is showing off a little. While the oysters are well in hand an hour ahead, their delicate butter sauce is made at the last moment. The wild mushrooms are also cooked for a very few minutes just before serving, while the pasta is cooking. The dessert is baked ahead, however, and served at room temperature. The recipes are not elaborate; where the cook is really showing off is in the choiceness of every ingredient.

4 slices thick-cut bacon, cut into 1-inch pieces
24 spinach leaves
24 fresh oysters, shucked and with their juices
2 cups clam juice
1 tablespoon lemon juice
1/2 teaspoon freshly ground white pepper
4 drops Tabasco sauce
4 tablespoons cold unsalted butter

Cook the bacon until crisp. Drain on paper towels and reserve.

Dip the spinach leaves in boiling water until wilted, about 5 seconds. Trim off the stems.

Combine the oyster and clam juices and bring to a boil. Reduce the heat to a simmer, add the oysters, and poach them until the edges curl, about 45 seconds. Reserve the liquid. Wrap each oyster in a spinach leaf and place three bundles in each of eight ramekins. At this point, the oysters can be held for 1 hour. Place the ramekins on a baking sheet and cover with aluminum foil.

Reduce the cooking liquid to 1/2 cup. Remove from the heat and add the lemon juice, white pepper, and Tabasco sauce. Whisk in the cold butter a bit at a time until you have an emulsified sauce.

While you are making the sauce, place the oyster bundles in a 250-degree oven for 5 minutes to reheat.

Spoon some sauce over each bundle and garnish with the pieces of bacon. Serve immediately.

SAUTEED WILD MUSHROOMS AND FETTUCCINE

3 pounds assorted wild mushrooms, such as cèpe, morel, girolle, Black Forest, oyster
2 pounds fresh fettuccine
12 tablespoons unsalted butter
1/2 cup white wine
1 1/2 cups heavy cream
1 teaspoon *glace de viande* (available commercially)
1/2 teaspoon freshly ground white pepper

Cut off the mushroom stems and save them for a stock or soup. If the mushrooms are large, cut them into bite-size pieces.

Start cooking the pasta and drain when al dente.

Meanwhile, sauté the mushrooms briefly in the butter, stir in the wine, cream, and seasonings and simmer until they are just wilted, about 6 minutes in all.

Serve the pasta on heated plates; top liberally with the mushrooms and spoon the sauce on top.

APPLE GALETTE

Homemade piecrust dough
4 large Granny Smith apples, peeled, cored, and sliced 1/4 inch thick
4 tablespoons unsalted butter, cut into small pieces
1/3 cup sugar

Preheat the oven to 400 degrees.

Use your favorite short crust recipe. Roll it out not quite 1/8 inch thick into a rectangle 14 by 18 inches and place on a 16- by 12-inch baking sheet.

Lay in the apple slices, overlapping them in rows and leaving a 1 1/2-inch border all around. Dot the apples with the butter. Fold over the pastry border and crimp it deeply. Sprinkle sugar over all and bake until dark brown and the apples have caramelized, about 45 minutes.

Let stand for 10 minutes before cutting into oblong slices. Serve at room temperature.

Note: It is a good idea to put a second baking sheet under the one holding the galette; this will prevent the bottom of the crust from scorching.

WINE *in* YOUR LIFE

Chapter Four

TASTING WINE & WINE TASTINGS

For anyone beginning to learn about wine, it may be helpful to point out that there is a significant difference between the act of tasting wine and the event known as a wine tasting. Tasting, as suggested earlier, can be part of everyday dining or of sipping an apéritif. It is an easily learned detective ritual that Sherlock Holmes would have classified as "elementary."

It begins not with the tongue, but with the eyes and nose. Once wine has been poured into your glass, look at it. The color and clarity, as with a person's eyes, may contain hints as to a wine's age and health. Generally, older wines have a duller color than young ones, and often ill-made wines will look cloudy or be of a color that is out of register.

The next step is to raise the glass to your lips. Stop right there.

One of the most extraordinary qualities of wine is that it has a distinctive smell (aroma and bouquet are the terms) that can vary markedly from one wine to another. It is an important part of the wine's personality. Therefore, while you have the wine in such an advantageous position—right under your nose, in fact—pause and take a sniff.

You may smell nothing. That happens. Even pedigreed wines can be "dumb." If you do smell something, and associations with flowers, fruits, or herbs leap to mind, you are taking the first step toward becoming a self-sufficient judge of wine. Try to file the sensation away. If there is a similar smell the next time you try this wine or another of the same type, you will remember. Coming to know wine is like learning a language—except that the sensations we receive in our nose and mouth translate very awkwardly into words. If you played in your grandmother's kitchen as a child while she was cooking, you may have retained strong associations that will come in handy. But for the moment, it is enough that the wine smell pleasing or, lacking that, intriguing.

Sniff and let yourself think briefly only about what you smell. That's all there is to it. There is no obligation to make associations, or to voice them if you do. Catching the bouquet of a wine can become a simple reflex action that helps you appreciate it and realize how different wine is from other beverages. But never be intimidated into believing there is a single, "correct" identity to the bouquet, no matter how insistent someone else may be. This is a personal and purely subjective exercise.

Now put some wine into your mouth. You can swallow it. That won't do any harm unless you swallow too much, too quickly. What will be more instructive, however, is to hold the wine in your mouth for several seconds. Roll it around your tongue. Breathe in a little air, if you wish. (The excusable slurping noise this may produce delights grown-ups who are still, at heart, children.)

At this point your taste buds will be challenged by sensations more varied than any other beverage offers them: Tartness (acidity), the possibility of bitterness, sweetness; the mouth can weigh the body of the wine, the length and complexity of what is called "finish." These impressions are recorded instinctively and very quickly. How consciously and how thoroughly depends on you.

This is where the wine tasting *event* comes in. It can be a very valuable training ground. You can learn the words for subjective descriptions of wine's characteristics, even technical terms; but until you taste (and sometimes even then, frankly), they are only words. Studying wine without tasting is like a science course without lab sessions or reading plays without ever attending the theater. You come to know wine by tasting it, and the best way to become informed is through organized tastings.

The reasons for taking up tastings can vary from simple curiosity to wanting a new social skill to a desire to make intelligent purchasing decisions on your own. Even if you taste casually and decide, for whatever reason, that you like wine #4 best, you will have accomplished something. Above all, tasting can be fun, an exercise, a game that never ends. There is such immense variety, so much variation from year to year, from producer to producer, and even vineyard to vineyard, that no one ever knows everything about wine.

Wine appreciation societies and tasting seminars are to be found in all parts of the country. If you want to hone your skills, join one or attend as a guest. You can, of course, taste wines by yourself. It's instructive, but in the long run it's about as satisfying as playing solitaire. One of the joys of drinking wine is sharing your reactions and talking about them. Therefore, it is much more interesting and pleasurable—as well as more economical—to participate in group tastings.

The home wine tasting can be as casual as sipping from a couple of bottles with your spouse or a friend on a weekend afternoon. Or it can be as formal as a black-tie affair with scorecards and wine waiters. The advantage, other than offering an opportunity to entertain friends, is that the home tasting can be personalized to suit your needs, degree of expertise, and depth of interest.

However, before you organize one, or start an informal tasting club that meets regularly, there are a few basic considerations that are worth remembering. First and foremost, don't try to achieve too much in a single

PRODUCE OF FRANCE

1981
Château Pichon
HAUT MEDOC
APPELLATION HAUT-MEDOC CONTROLEE

SOCIÉTÉ DES VIGNOBLES DOMINIQUE PICHON
PROPRIETAIRE A PAREMPUYRE MEDOC

75cl

MIS EN BOUTEILLE AU CHATEAU

CREATION GIP LIBOURNE ©

tasting. There should be a structure: wines of the same grape type, or of the same region, or of the same vintage. The number of wines to be tasted should be limited. Half a dozen is plenty, unless the tasters are all experienced and you have unlimited time.

Someone should lead the tasting. It can be you, an experienced friend, or, perhaps, a wine merchant you deal with. As long as you have the requisite number of glasses, the number of participants doesn't matter. A single bottle will yield a dozen tasting portions, and it is common practice to divide up the task of obtaining wines and the cost of them.

In the long run, a tasting can only offer you the opportunity to compare wines and recognize them through analysis—Sherlock Holmes again. It's work, so to be meaningful, the tasting should be conducted with a minimum of distraction—in a room away from household traffic and superfluous noise. Everyone should be given something to write with and paper, notepads or formal scoring sheets to record impressions. Recall is fleeting when you taste several similar wines, and it helps to have notes in front of you when the general review begins. The host should also provide receptacles for wine that is spit out (a surprisingly few swallows will dull your tasting sensitivity) and bread or unsalted crackers. Those are the essentials. A wine tasting is much easier to orchestrate than a meal with wine.

If the tasting is a serious one, you will want to ensure good light (fluorescent bulbs may distort a wine's color) and provide a white tablecloth or mats. It's also helpful to number the glasses, or the position of the glasses at each place. Finally, serve the wines at a warmer temperature than you would with a meal. Their characteristics become more obvious when they are not cold.

And then there is "blind tasting," which means simply that the bottles have been masked, or decanted into numbered containers, so that their identities are not known. Like justice, subjective wine tasting is better done blind. The object is not to dissemble; the tasters should know, in general, what is before them. But anyone who has ever seen the price of a bottle of Château Lafite-Rothschild or another classic wine cannot help but be impressed at the sight of its label. Conversely, the taster may be instinctively prejudiced against a popularly priced wine from a large producer.

So that everyone can play on more or less equal terms, tasters sometimes employ a "double-blind"

technique. One person uncorks the bottles and either covers them with paper bags or decants them, recording the names in sequence. A second person numbers the wines randomly, recording this sequence. Then no one knows exactly which wine is which until numbers and names are paired at the conclusion of the tasting.

The benefit of tastings is that they enable you to judge wines against their peers at a single sitting instead of making evaluations in the abstract—as you must do if you taste a chardonnay in a restaurant and then try another at home two weeks or a month later. It also allows you to learn by comparing your impressions with those of other tasters with more experience—or for that matter, less experience. Listen and learn, but don't fall under the spell of the most confident, articulate person present. Keep your own reactions in mind and learn to trust them.

Professional wine tasters prefer to do their analysis in the early morning. As a certified amateur, you can combine the business of tasting with pleasure by holding your event before a lunch or dinner. Then the discussion can merge into convivial conversation and the remaining wine can be poured and drunk for pure pleasure.

THE WINE & CHEESE PARTY

Offering cheese with wine is one of the oldest and simplest feasts of food and wine. It's also one of the safest and easiest ways to be social. Almost everyone likes cheese, and with so many of the world's fine cheeses easily accessible these days, there is a nearly endless variety to put forth. Wine, in turn, sparkles at a party. It's no surprise, then, that wine and cheese parties have become an American institution, a favorite form of entertaining in offices as well as homes, and have civilized the staple hotel or club reception.

Their appeal to the host or hostess is obvious: Wine and cheese parties require no elaborate preparation and have only three essential components, cheese, wine, and bread or crackers. Guests serve themselves, can come and go over a period of time, and leftovers will keep for use later.

If there is a single drawback, it is that their popularity has made them something of a cliché. How to stage the party is a less difficult challenge than how to make it your own. The key to success, I've found, is always to remember that the cheese and wine party is,

first and foremost, a party. The most important ingredient is lively conversation. Don't try to over-glamorize the occasion with splendid but difficult-to-appreciate wines. Instead, personalize it by selecting attractive, pleasant-drinking wines of character along with appropriate cheeses. Then anyone, including people unfamiliar with wine, can share the joy of discovery. And they will, as you will find out when you receive numerous requests for where to buy one or another of the wines.

In many states, you need look no farther than the supermarket to obtain the essentials, and not costly ones. Jugs of wine, French bread and firm, easy-to-cut cheeses are appropriate. It's more fun, of course, to stock up at good specialty shops. While red wine is the traditional partner of cheese, so many Americans prefer white wine these days that both should be served. There is, in fact, no shortage of cheeses that are delightful companions to white wine. The whites should be cold and the reds should be chilled as they will warm up rather quickly unless you keep them on ice. If you are using jug wines, you do need someone on hand to pour because of the size and weight of the bottles. Alternatively, pour the wine into carafes.

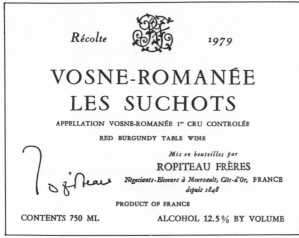

Récolte 1979

VOSNE-ROMANÉE LES SUCHOTS

APPELLATION VOSNE-ROMANÉE 1ᵉʳ CRU CONTRÔLÉE

RED BURGUNDY TABLE WINE

Mis en bouteilles par
ROPITEAU FRÈRES
Négociants-Eleveurs à Meursault, Côte-d'Or, FRANCE
depuis 1848
PRODUCT OF FRANCE

CONTENTS 750 ML   ALCOHOL 12.5% BY VOLUME

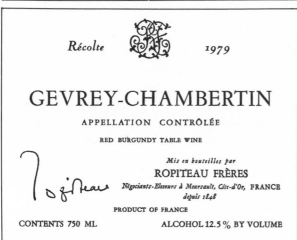

Récolte 1979

GEVREY-CHAMBERTIN

APPELLATION CONTRÔLÉE

RED BURGUNDY TABLE WINE

Mis en bouteilles par
ROPITEAU FRÈRES
Négociants-Eleveurs à Meursault, Côte-d'Or, FRANCE
depuis 1848
PRODUCT OF FRANCE

CONTENTS 750 ML   ALCOHOL 12.5% BY VOLUME

Ancien Domaine des TEMPLIERS

1974
CHÂTEAU GAZIN
POMEROL

APPELLATION POMEROL CONTROLÉE

*Mise en bouteilles
du Château*

73cl

· E. de BAILLIENCOURT, Prᵉ - 33 - POMEROL ·

MODÈLE DÉPOSÉ   PRODUCE OF FRANCE   GIP-LIBOURNE

As this is a party, not a structured tasting, I limit the choices. I find that offering more than half a dozen selections of wines and of cheeses leads to confusion and is ultimately wasteful. An extensive presentation, which can be very instructive, is best reserved for a sit-down tasting of cheese with wine for a small group. I prefer to separate the red wines and the white, each with their own cheeses. At the white table there may be two wines and three cheeses—no more—and the same at the red table. This two-table formula works well for up to twenty persons. As the numbers increase, simply add more tables that duplicate the selections on the originals. Set up the tables in well-scattered spots to encourage your guests to circulate. You can serve all the wine at a bar and have the guests move on to the cheese selection, but I prefer to suggest the best pairings by keeping the wines and cheeses together.

Provisioning a wine and cheese party is delightfully uncomplicated. Plan on one quarter pound of cheese and one third bottle of wine for each guest. Therefore, for a dozen persons, three pounds of cheese and four bottles of wine will do very well. (Extra back-up bottles are good for the host's peace of mind.) Unless the party is a special event, glassware is not important. Mix and match, or place glasses of different sizes and shapes at different tables.

Aim to make things as easy as possible for your guests. Be sure there are knives enough for all the cheeses. If a cheese is difficult to cut, or should be sliced in a special way, precut some of it to show how it should be done and encourage people to try it. For example, Parmesan, the hardest of all cheeses, is an excellent companion to red wine, but is very difficult to cut. Serve it with the special trowel-like knife that breaks off small nuggets. At the other extreme, avoid ripe soft cheeses, such as Brie, because they will run when they become warm. Ideally, to serve them and other delicate varieties, what's needed is a cheese and bread tender—just like a bartender—to cut and slice as required.

To provide an additional dimension, as decoration or for eating, use apples, pears, and grapes with the cheese selection. Supplement the cheese with unsalted nuts and celery sticks. If the trays or boards on which the cheeses are presented are of wood, marble, or straw, they will add a stylish touch to the display.

If the party is scheduled outside the late-afternoon, early-evening "cocktail" period, after the theater or a concert for instance, I will enlarge the "menu" by introducing cheese-based hors-d'oeuvre. I may also serve a dessert wine with a suitable cheese and possibly a sweet. Among hors-d'oeuvre to consider are cheese straws, open-face hot or cold cheese sandwiches, and quiche or croquettes. With dessert wine, blue-veined and some other salty cheeses match very well, as will a not-too-sweet cheesecake. Port and Stilton are classics together.

As a wine lover, you will be concerned that the cheeses suit the wines well and do not detract from their qualities. Considering that the distractions of parties do preclude deep concentration, it is enough to think in terms of types of cheese and wine rather than specific pairings. Or a theme concept can organize what you do—such as wines and cheeses from the same country or region. A conversation piece like a new Beaujolais or other nouveau wine can't miss and loves a good cheese.

The following suggested pairings should nevertheless be helpful. They lean toward wines and cheeses with like characteristics—similarly pronounced aromas or equally mild flavors—and they refer you back to the Wine Selection Chart on page 16.

Goats'-milk cheeses: red or white Inside Circle wines.

Buttery cheeses, such as Edam and Monterey Jack: Middle Circle red, blush, or Middle Circle white wines.

Soft-ripened cheeses, such as Brie, Camembert, Reblochon: Middle Circle red wines.

Double- and triple-crème cheeses, such as Explorateur, Saint-André, Bellétoile: mature Outside Circle red wines, sweet wines, or cream sherry.

Blue-veined cheeses: sweet white wines, Outside Circle reds, Port.

Semisoft cheeses, such as Port-du-Salut or St. Paulin: Middle Circle red or white wines.

Semihard cheeses, such as Swiss varieties and Gruyère: Middle Circle red, blush, or Middle Circle white wines, especially Chardonnay.

Cheddar cheeses: red Middle Circle.

APÉRITIFS

What to drink before a meal, especially a feast of wine and food? Once upon a time nothing was offered. At the appointed hour, people just sat down and ate. Customs change, however, and for a time in our country the pendulum swung so far that the cocktail "hour" tended to last longer than dinner. Spirits, not wine, were the beverage of choice, and because of their strength, many people chose to forego wine with the meal that followed. To deal with hunger and counteract the effects of several cocktails, hosts and hostesses would "pour on" the hors-d'oeuvre, serving miniature meals that made the meal that followed anticlimactic.

Of late, the trend has been to serve wine or wine-based beverages before the meal, as an alternative to spirits, or, perhaps, in place of them. We've cut back on pass-around appetizers, too, thus making the dining table the focus of the occasion once again. During the inevitable wait for late-comers, bottled water and fruit juice are no longer just mixers, they are popular cocktail substitutes.

A clue to what wines to serve at this time comes from the word itself. Translated from the French, *apéritif* means appetizer, something to stimulate the appetite. (Wine, it should be noted, also stimulates conversation and the ritual of pouring, passing, and drinking it helps relieve the awkwardness that is common when a social gathering begins.)

For me, the ideal apéritif is cool, tart or no more than mildly sweet, and contains some titillating bubbles. In a word, champagne or, in two words, sparkling wine. All champagne sparkles, but the French contend that only sparkling wine made in the region called Champagne should bear that name. Sparkling wine of whatever origin is festive and fun, thirst-quenching and intriguing, the ideal extra guest. Pouring even French Champagne seems much more extravagant than it is. Its bubbles carry a subliminal message of gaiety and announce clearly that your guests are at a party, a special occasion.

When selecting a champagne to serve as an apéritif, look for the designation "brut" on the label. That indicates that the wine will be medium-dry, neither cloying like "champagne" you may have encountered at receptions nor so tart it makes your lips pucker. Quality champagne is made in the United States as well as France. Prices vary sharply and there are marked differences in taste from one brand to another. Experiment until you find one that pleases you; then keep some on hand, chilled.

Still white wine, well chilled or served with ice and soda water as a spritzer, is useful as an apéritif. For a small group, you may want to pour the same wine that will be served with the first course. I don't, however, risk disappointment later by serving my best wine before the meal begins. Sometimes a fruit syrup or liqueur is added to white wine to make a pretty colored, fragrant apéritif. If *crème de cassis* is used, the drink is called a Kir. Practice before serving them to company, as the syrup is intensely sweet and can easily overwhelm the wine. Start with only a teaspoon per glass and add syrup until the balance suits you. Then remember the resulting color as a reference for the future. Among dry white wines that are well suited to being served as apéritifs are American chablis, Fumé Blanc, Chenin Blanc; French Macon or Beaujolais blanc, Sancerre, Entre-Deux-Mers from Bordeaux; Italian Soave, Verdicchio.

Slightly sweet riesling wines from Germany or California are wonderful apéritifs, especially in warm weather when their crisp freshness is as welcome as a bite of chilled fruit. If no hors-d'oeuvre are to be served, the rieslings have no difficulty holding center stage as a solo act. Rosé and "blush" wines can be appealing to drink by themselves, too, but be sure the one you serve does not taste sweet and has no more than 12 degrees or so of alcohol.

Another of the world's great apéritifs is a wine name that comes easily to everyone's lips, but is too seldom drunk in this country—sherry. Sherry tastes brown and rich, and contains more alcohol than table wine, enough to explain why it is served in small glasses. There's nothing neutral about sherry. It has character, distinctive aroma, and a lingering taste. Don't assume it will please everyone. Seek out a dry Fino or the nutty, fuller-flavored Amontillado and chill them. Sherry's natural companions are food native to Spain, notably almonds and olives, as well as egg appetizers, smoked fish, and smoked poultry.

Everywhere but in the United States—where over the years people have made a fetish of allowing as little of it as possible gain access to a martini cocktail—vermouth is an important apéritif. It is wine that has been fortified with brandy and seasoned with mysterious combinations of herbs and spices that vary from one manufacturer to another. Red vermouths are markedly sweet. There are also more than half a dozen brand-name apéritifs imported from Italy and France that are made with vermouth or in a similar fashion. They have

names such as Dubonnet, Lillet, Campari.

There is no need to present guests with a broad assortment of apéritifs, however. Those who won't drink champagne or sherry, for instance, will probably be content with a glass of still wine or sparkling water. As for hors-d'oeuvre, when re-creating the menus in this book, I recommend that you serve a minimum. Your guests won't grumble once they are aware of the feast ahead.

DESSERT WINES

Dessert wines are, by and large, wonderful creations. They can provide a honeyed bouquet and taste, "ambrosia" the ancients called it, to help end a meal with a smile. Serve them with dessert, or by themselves *as* dessert. You needn't pour much. A three- or even a two-ounce portion of these rich wines usually is sufficient, and after even one sip the aroma and flavor will linger in your memory.

The term "dessert wine" causes confusion. In the context of this book, it means simply a wine to serve with dessert. The U.S. Government has a narrower definition: a wine that contains between 14 and 21 percent alcohol. Most of the wines recommended with our feasts of food and wine have considerably less alcohol. Dessert wines also cause apprehension. It is one of the anomalies of our time that, despite the almost certain pleasure they bring to those who taste them, dessert wines are hard to sell in the United States.

Perhaps part of the cause is a lingering perception of Skid Row drunks downing cheap muscatel, sherry, and "sauterne." But the major handicap seems to be that they are sweet, and we Americans become skittish when we are told a wine is not "dry." Although we crave sugar or sugar substitutes in our coffee, tea, and soft drinks, we have developed a blind prejudice against wines that contain what the chemists call "residual sugar." (This is grape sugar that remains in the wine after the fermentation process has been completed or intentionally stopped. It becomes noticeable when in excess of 1 percent and may go as high as 33 percent in such intensely sweet wines as the Trockenbeerenauslese of Germany.)

Somehow, in an era of thinking thin, diet, and exercise, desserts have found new popularity. The same should happen to dessert wines. In fact, the sweet wines used interchangeably for apéritifs and with some desserts, which the trade prefers to call "off-dry," really are not very sugary. Add a couple of teaspoons of you-know-what to a six-ounce cup of coffee and you will create a beverage with more residual sugar than

these wines contain. The ante moves up with Sauternes and other liquorous wines. They have a good deal more residual sugar, but when they are properly made there is a healthy balance between this sugar and acidity. The lack of demand for them is something of a blessing. The finest examples are hand-crafted, remarkably complex, and extremely expensive to produce. They cannot be made in great quantity, so if they became as fashionable today as they were in earlier eras, prices would soar. The problem is finding them in retail stores, but it's worth the search as you will find some very stylish wines at bargain prices.

There are three categories of wine suggested with desserts in this book: sparkling, late harvest, and fortified.

Once sparkling champagne was a sweet wine reserved for dessert and post-meal sipping and toasts. Sweet champagne is rare these days, but wines in the "demi-sec" category (which means semi-sweet, not semi-dry) will prove excellent companions for many pastries, fruit desserts, mousses and sweet cakes. Look to California, the Asti region of Italy, the Loire Valley in France and Champagne itself for the best of these wines. When the dessert is not too sugary, cookies and dry cakes for instance, all but the very driest sparkling wines are satisfactory.

Late harvest wines (Spätlese in German), are made mostly from white grapes left on the vine until the sugar content has risen appreciably beyond the norm. It's a risky business. The grapes are overripe. Weather and disease threaten. The quantity of wine obtained will be less. But in select regions there is a chance that a mold called the "noble rot" (Botrytis cinerea) will attack the grapes. It causes the grapes to lose water and shrink, thus concentrating the sugar and making it possible to vinify exceptionally sweet, rich wines. This process occurs, though not invariably, with the Sauternes and Barsacs of Bordeaux and various wines from Alsace and the Loire valleys in France; the auslese wines of Germany; Tokay in Hungary; muscat wines in Italy (such as Moscato di Canelli, Vin Santo), and riesling, sauvignon, semillon, muscat canelli and even zinfandel wines in California. As weather conditions are so important to the creation of late harvest wines, vintage is a very important factor in choosing them. A bargain price may be a sign of an inferior year. Do some homework before you buy.

Fortified wine is a forbidden term in the U.S. Government lexicon, a holdover from Prohibition. Nonetheless, it accurately describes what happens in the process of producing the luscious Ports, cream sherries, and some muscat wines. Fermentation is stopped before all the sugar has converted to alcohol. Then brandy is added to bring the alcohol level up to about 20 percent. The wine is then aged and bottled. Many people prefer to drink these wines on their own, apart from a meal, but they do well with full-flavored desserts. Cream sherry will complement a nut-filled dessert, Port is a traditional companion for Stilton or other blue-veined cheeses as well as English trifle. Muscats do best with fruit desserts and dry cakes. All these wines keep for a relatively long time, even after they have been opened.

COOKING WITH WINE

Consider wine as simply the liquid in a recipe, and most of the mystique about cooking with it evaporates. In other words, if there is no wine available, you can use stock or even water and make the recipe successfully—but it tastes better if you use wine. In addition to taste, wine's assets in flavoring food are its acid, sugar, and alcohol contents. Wine adds character to any cooking liquid, soup, or sauce. Red wine can impart color, and both red and white wines act as tenderizing agents in marinades.

Wine works—as easily as if it had been made for them—in each of the basic moist-heat methods of cooking. In braising and stewing, the wine mellows and strengthens the juices during the long cooking times. For flavor in poaching and steaming, *court-bouillon,* which French cooks invented for the brief cooking of fish and seafood, is merely a mix—usually fifty/fifty to be effective—of wine and water, made aromatic also with vegetables and herbs. And wine can be used to baste a roast, or a fish baked in the oven, yielding pan juices that are the sauce for the dish.

It is a safe bet that any favorite basic recipe you use that requires liquid for cooking meat, poultry, or fish will be improved if you substitute wine for a fourth to a half of the liquid called for. Beef needs red wine. White wine is best for veal and fish if you are experimenting. Chicken will happily soak up either one.

Best of all, for the cook in a hurry, is using wine to make an instant pan sauce. This simple technique is a favorite of restaurant chefs because it is ideal for dishes made to order. For exactly the same reason, it works for the home cook. The pan sauce is the end result of "deglazing," and it works for any meats, from the simple hamburger to chops to choice veal scallops, cooked in a frying pan.

Remove the meat once it is cooked, add (for two servings) 1/4 cup of red or white wine to the pan. Return the pan to the heat and, as the wine boils, scrape the bottom of the pan to loosen the meat particles and extracts stuck to the surface. This is deglazing. When the mixture has reduced enough to turn slightly syrupy, stir in a pat of butter and immediately pour this liquid—your sauce—over the meat. *"Voilà!"* as the French are wont to say. There are, of course, all sorts of variations. You can use stock in combination with the wine, and season the liquid with salt, pepper and fresh herbs. But the process itself is that simple and produces one of the best flavor payoffs—considering the minimal time and effort—in all of cooking.

Because of the small amount of wine needed to deglaze a pan, it may be more convenient to use dry vermouth from an already open bottle that is sitting around waiting for a martini-drinker to appear. Otherwise, just pour off the requisite amount of wine from the bottle you'll be drinking with the meal.

Another way to utilize the flavor of concentrated wine is to reduce it with herbs or shallots as the first step in making a sauce. Cook down wine with tarragon and you are on your way to making a béarnaise sauce. A wine and shallot reduction is the first step in making a classic *beurre blanc*. Let the reduction cool and you can use it to flavor mayonnaise. Paul Bocuse, the great French chef, even uses Beaujolais in place of vinegar to create a salad dressing that is compatible with wine.

When you want a mellow marinade, use wine in place of vinegar, or sometimes in combination with it. Strained and cooked down, these marinades can become deliciously rich sauces. Wine even finds its way into barbecue sauce recipes.

The cooking methods just described usually call for dry wines, but sweet wines have their uses in the kitchen, too. They marry well with fruit, will enhance the flavor of a sorbet, a soufflé, or a fruit or custard sauce. I keep sweet wines in mind, as well, for sauces destined to accompany sweet-compatible meats, such as pork, ham, duck, or calf's liver.

There are a number of minor stipulations about cooking with wine, but the important warning that cannot be repeated often enough has always been: If a wine is not of good enough quality to drink, do not cook with it. Products sold as "cooking wine" are generally of inferior character and invariably have been seasoned with salt. Ignore them in favor of reasonably priced jug wines. My own experiments have convinced me that using a great wine in cooking is rarely worth the expense. Sometimes, in fact, these wine are too refined to produce an identifiable aroma or flavor, especially in long-cooking dishes.

Of less moment, but worth remembering, is that wine may have a chemical reaction with aluminum cookware because of its acid content. A bitter taste may result. Aluminum also may cause red wine to turn an embarassingly unappetizing color.

If you add wine early to a long-cooking dish, such as a stew, the alcohol will evaporate of its own accord. If you add it only minutes before serving, the wine should be flamed first or boiled intensely to rid it of its alcohol. This is not a Prohibitionist sentiment. When heated, alcohol turns bitter and can impart an unpleasant taste to food. If the wine is to be mixed with stock or another liquid, you will accomplish this exorcism more easily if you heat the wine separately and then flame it before mixing. Otherwise the diluted wine may not burn.

Leftover wine is a likely candidate for cooking, even if it has lost the freshness that makes it a delight to drink. Taste the wine before using it, however, to make sure its spirit and flavor have not departed totally.

Almaden
CARAFE CHABLIS
OF CALIFORNIA

VINTED AND BOTTLED BY ALMADEN VINEYARDS
SAN JOSE, CA   ALCOHOL 11.5%
BY VOLUME

VINEGAR

You won't find much information about vinegar in most wine texts. For wine makers, vinegar is an enemy. But for cooks it is a wonderful tool, and can be the "secret" ingredient that makes a salad dressing or sauce memorable. I'm bringing the subject to your attention for a simple reason: Inevitably your feasts of wine and food will give you, as a by-product so to speak, a supply of the essential raw material for the best of all vinegars—leftover wine.

The style, type and quality of vinegars vary greatly. Most supermarket vinegars are too harsh and acidic. They afford bite but no pleasure. The vinegars you make at home will be mild, subtle, and almost sweet enough to sip.

At the most primitive level, you can simply leave wine in the open bottle. Prolonged exposure to the air will oxidize the wine and turn it into a vinegar of sorts. But don't bet that it will be wonderful, or even satisfactory. As with all handcrafted products, the best doesn't just happen. You will do better if you aid the process by using a commercial powdered wine mother or natural wine vinegar. (Avoid any vinegar labeled "distilled.") The wine can be either white or red. It should not, however, be sterilized or stabilized, as many jug wines are. Nor will the chemistry be right if you use fortified wines. Standard good table wine is what you need and better-quality wine will give you a more distinctive vinegar.

The wine and the vinegar or mother should be combined in a sterilized, wide-mouthed bottle. Fill the bottle not more than half full, cover it with cheesecloth and leave it undisturbed in a comfortable (60- to 75-degree) place for several weeks. Once you have a vinegar (tasting will tell you when), try to draw off and replenish the supply in roughly equal amounts. You can season drawn-off vinegar with herbs and spices as you see fit, but don't mess with the central reservoir.

There is a delightfully iconoclastic discourse on more complex and exotic homemade vinegars in Richard Olney's *Simple French Food* (David Godine). You will also find advertisements for vinegar-making kits in specialty food magazines. Lastly, and perhaps the simplest method of all if you consume only limited amounts of either wine or vinegar, you might want to buy a small wooden vinegar barrel that comes with a store of red or white wine vinegar of good quality already inside. Simply add wine in proportion to the amount of vinegar you take out. These, too, are advertised in specialty publications and mail-order catalogues.

SHOPPING FOR WINE

"Where there is no choice," someone wryly observed, "you have no problem." If there is only a single source of wine near you, so be it. If there are several, you probably will do your shopping based on convenience, price, selection and service. For day-to-day drinking that's fine. The order of priorities should be reversed, however, when your goals are to learn more about wine and to begin, or expand, a collection. Then no bargain will be worth as much as the advice and counsel of a knowledgeable wine merchant. It's money in your pocket and wine of better quality on your table if you make the effort to search out and cultivate one.

To begin, once you have his attention, describe your level of knowledge and your areas of interest. Ask him to recommend a sampling of bottles within these perimeters, take them home and try them. When you return, seek out the same person, describe your reaction to the wines and ask for further recommendations. If he or she takes an interest, and if the new wines suit you, a rapport has been established. If there's no chemistry, keep trying until you find a merchant who does respond.

As for wine departments and shops, it doesn't take much experience to size one up. The best have more than the nationally advertised brands on display. There will be a wide-ranging selection with wines from older vintages as well as the more recent. The store may emphasize wines of one region or country, California or Bordeaux or Italy. Prices probably will not be cut-rate, but within each category you should find some bargains. Often good shops will sponsor tastings or publish a newsletter. If a cheese department is attached to the store, so much the better.

As people become more self-sufficient in selecting wine, they tend to do more comparison shopping and may attend auctions or buy wine futures (purchasing wine of an outstanding vintage before it has been aged and bottled). Even then, the basic shopping tips apply. Buy in quantity only wines that you like to drink and that match up with foods you like to eat. (Many expensive and exotic wines remain unopened forever because there is rarely an occasion to drink that type of wine.) Buy in small amounts when experimenting or trying to expand your horizons. Stick to producers and vineyards that please you. Their wines become friends and often, in less than remarkable vintages, may reward you with something special at a bargain price.

It's up to you to establish a price–value relationship. In Bordeaux, the price of the classified first growth wines is at least double the price of the second growths in any given vintage and may be several times that of the lesser growths. Rarely, if ever, is the quality spread equally great. Often it becomes a question of investing in a prestige label, but, to repeat an observation offered earlier, you will never truly enjoy a wine you think you paid too much for. At other points on the price spectrum, the little bargain wine may never be more than that, while for a few dollars more you might purchase a wine with the potential to be memorable.

The choices are ours to make. Remember that buying wine can become an obsession and try not to let your purchases too greatly outnumber the bottles you consume. Lastly, learn not to be stampeded into buying quantities of wine from the most recent "vintage of the century." There will be another one along in a very few years. In the meantime, you may be surprised how many sold-out wines from the celebrated vintage resurface as time passes.

WINE STORAGE

This may seem to be heresy, but like many other subjects dear to wine buffs, storage is of minimal concern to the average wine drinker. Simply put, you do not need a wine cellar unless you intend to become a wine collector. Today's wines are remarkably stable and resilient compared to those of years ago. Today's homes and apartments are notably smaller than the mansions of the past where aristocrats laid down wine to be opened by their children and grandchildren. For many of us, a wine cellar is not a practical consideration.

The essential question to ask yourself, then, is how much wine do you plan to store and for how long. Almost every element that threatens wine in the long term is not going to do appreciable harm if the period of storage is a year or less. During that period of time, wine will survive very well in the same environment we live in. Keep the bottles on their sides where they won't be jarred or need to be moved often, at a fairly stable temperature and away from direct sunlight. That's all there is to it.

If the amount of wine on hand grows to more than a

MIS EN BOUTEILLE AU CHATEAU

Chateau Lalande-Borie

SAINT-JULIEN

APPELLATION SAINT-JULIEN CONTROLÉE

1983

JEAN-EUGÈNE BORIE, PROPRIÉTAIRE A St-JULIEN-BEYCHEVELLE (GIRONDE)

PRODUCE OF FRANCE   75cl

couple of cases, a storage rack or racks becomes useful because it makes access to individual bottles much easier. Beyond that lie the temptations to buy more and better that accompany any hobby: a closet, a separate room, even a vault that's air conditioned and humidity-controlled with custom-built racks, a cellar book and perhaps even a table for tastings. With money, it's all available and so are the many vintages of the world's great wines. If wine collecting becomes a passion, you can be certain of this: The amount of wine you purchase will exceed your projections and your storage capacity.

WINE IN RESTAURANTS

Restaurants offer great potential for learning about wine and enjoying it with friends. A good wine list is as stimulating as the display in a candystore. You can choose from among a broad array of wines from many countries, of many types and vintages, at a wide range of price. You can watch the serving technique of an expert wine waiter and learn how to pronounce some of those hard-to-grasp names. You can discover memorable wine and food combinations. You can take home the label of a wine that has impressed you and seek it out at your local shop. Most of all, you will be convinced time and again that wine adds immeasurably to the conviviality and pleasure of a meal.

The wine list tells a great deal about a restaurant. Ideally, it should be up-to-date, easy to read, and clearly distinguish among wine regions and grape types. To be truly helpful, the list needs to contain the vintage date of a wine and the producer in addition to the name. Display and organization can vary greatly, from books that contain maps and actual labels to computer printouts.

Whatever may be is missing from the list, there are always prices and they are often confusing. Wine pricing in restaurants is mysterious. In general, the imagination—or lack of it—in the selection and the prices are reflections of how much or little an owner respects wine and his customers. There are formulas for pricing, but restaurateurs find countless rationales for markups that are higher, and occasionally lower, than the norm.

While the trend is by no means universal, many of the restaurants across the United States that offer wine have become noticeably more sophisticated in their selection and marketing. Wine bars, which sell wine by

the glass, exist in most major cities today, and more and more restaurants are dramatically increasing the options available to customers by selling wines this way as well as by the bottle. In such a situation, especially when a dispenser is used to keep wine fresh under a cap of nitrogen once it has been opened, all sorts of comparisons are possible. You can indulge in comparative tastings for less money and effort than you would expend doing them at home. Also, the conundrum of what wine to choose when one person orders meat and the other fish disappears. Each person can have a different wine.

As for the wine list, with experience a brief scan is sufficient to reveal whether it has a stock selection or, with luck, tempting choices. But no list, no matter how carefully prepared, can tell all you need to know. If the gods are smiling, the waiter will provide the rest.

A wine waiter, if he or she is on top of the job, will know which wines are "drinking well," which have passed their prime, and often can suggest an intriguing match for the food you are ordering. Once the selection and tasting rituals have been completed, he also will return frequently enough to keep wine in each glass. If the waiter suggests something that exceeds your budget, you are the customer. Simply say you prefer something less costly. Any suggestion can be politely rejected, but if you have strong preferences or prejudices, it is only fair to state them at the beginning of the discussion.

In a great many restaurants, even some very fancy ones, there is no designated wine waiter or sommelier. The staff take wine orders as part of their serving duties. If the waiter's lack of knowledge is immediately apparent, ask if there is someone available who is a wine specialist. If not, the best course is to opt for a moderately priced wine with which you are familiar.

In any situation, the following thoughts about dealing with wine and wine service in restaurants are ones I keep in mind:

• Ask for the wine list as soon as you arrive. It may suggest an apéritif wine. Also, you will have time for study while food choices are being discussed.

• Before ordering, it's a good idea to mention the name of a wine—or wines—that appeals to you to the waiter. He then knows your area of interest and an acceptable price range and can respond by approving your nominee or suggesting alternatives. If you know exactly what you want, you do others a favor by ordering it straightaway. This will free the wine waiter, like a doctor or priest, to be of service where he is needed.

• Be wary of a "great" vintage, especially if the wine is red and the year is recent. Wine of these famous years tend to mature slowly and may be tannic and harsh if drunk young. Wine from less acclaimed years, "restaurant vintages" the trade calls them, may be more pleasant to drink and better suited to your meal.

• Be equally wary of ordering "great" old wines in restaurants. It's uncertain how long and how well the bottle has been stored on these premises. Many restaurants will not take responsibility for the quality of these

RHEINGAU 750 ml
Qualitätswein mit Prädikat
A. P. Nr. 34 003 011 84
1983er Kiedricher Gräfenberg
Riesling Kabinett
Erzeugerabfüllung aus dem Weingut des
Dr. R. Weil, Kiedrich/Rheingau

Produce of Germany

TURMBERG

WOLF, ELTVILLE

antiques and even red wines of less than venerable ages are likely to become clouded with sediment if they are not properly served. If you have your eye on an old wine from a restaurant's list you are familiar with, consider ordering it when you make your reservation. Then the bottle can be stood upright and brought to the proper temperature before your arrival.

• In determining how much wine to order, remember that unless the waiter is inexperienced or trying to force a second bottle on the table, he will pour so that a bottle provides six servings. Half-bottles of dessert wines will yield four servings.

• It's wise to take a moment to read the label when a wine is presented. More often than it should, an error will occur and the wine will be of a more recent vintage than the one marked on the list, from another producer or shipper, or occasionally it may be a different wine altogether. It's our prerogative to send the bottle back and, if we wish, change the order. If the bottle has been opened already, too bad. Restaurant etiquette dictates that the bottle be opened in front of the customer after he or she approves the selection.

• The tasting ritual is done for your benefit. Take your time. You can swirl the wine in the glass. Smell, taste, and think for a moment. The waiter has to wait for you and he's not giving a test. If the wine is bad enough to be sent back, it should be obvious. Bad bottles are fairly rare and wine waiters and owners who resist taking them back are even more rare. As long as a customer does not create a scene, a management

proud of its wine list will not create a problem for its customer.

• If red wine has been ordered for the main course, it is perfectly appropriate to ask that it be poured into glasses as soon as it has been opened. This will allow increased exposure to the air and should make the wine more ready to drink when its turn comes.

• Most restaurants keep chilled white wine on hand, so the long delays while wine chills down are rare these days. But sometimes sticking a well-chilled white wine into an ice bucket will make it too cold. I don't hesitate to ask that it be removed, or to remove it myself if the waiter has disappeared. Conversely, at the room temperature in many restaurants, you may want to ask that your red wine, even a fine one, be put in the ice bucket for five minutes or so to bring it to a more refreshing temperature.

• Tipping for wine service is not difficult in restaurants where the waiter also performs the sommelier's chores. The wine charges probably will be part of the total bill and tipping the normal percentage on the total will be appropriate. Where there is a wine waiter and he accords special service, a separate cash tip is in order, perhaps $5 for a wine costing up to $50 and proportionately more above that. I usually refrain from this gesture if the wine server is the owner of the restaurant. If the waiter is enthusiastic about wine, another way to reward him if the wine is special, is to leave some in the bottle expressly for him. From such gestures are friendships born.

BOTTLE SHAPES & SIZES

In the world of wine, the shape of a bottle is a tip-off to what's inside. There are only half a dozen shapes for the bottles that hold most of the wine you will see on the shelves of a retail shop. (See page 14.)

The most complex design belongs to the long-necked bottle used for Champagne and other sparkling wines. Due to the pressure within the bottle—up to 90 pounds per square inch—more glass is used and an indentation, or punt, is built into the bottom of the bottle to strengthen it. Champagne bottles are heavy.

The Burgundy bottle, used for both red and white wines, including Chardonnays and Pinot Noirs made in this country, is a scaled-down, flat-bottomed version of the Champagne bottle. Stocky, with broad sloping shoulders, it looks squat, but in fact is the same height as the more elegant, square-shouldered Bordeaux bottle. This latter shape is used for both reds (green bottle) and whites (clear bottle) from Bordeaux and in most other wine regions of France as well, in Chianti and Piedmont in Italy, in Spain's Rioja, for Sauvignon Blanc and other white wines in California, and anywhere in the world where Cabernet Sauvignon is produced.

Far less common is the tall, gracefully slender bottle the Germans use for their white wines. If the bottle is brown, the wine most likely comes from the Rhine River valley; if green, from the Moselle River valley. The white wines of Alsace are sold in similarly shaped bottles, as are Reisling wines made in many countries including the United States.

Among the most unusual is the wide-based, narrow bottle with a shape like an inverted ping-pong paddle that is used in Portugal and Germany's Franconia region. This distinctive shape, blown up to two or three times the original size, holds the American jug wines of Almaden. Bottles for other jug wines made in this country and in Europe tend to be broad and square-shouldered. Sherry and Port come in long-necked bottles of dark glass, while vermouths are sold in a more barrel-chested variation on the Bordeaux bottle.

The amount of wine that can be poured into the bottles of various sizes sold in the United States is strictly regulated by law and became far easier to understand when the United States switched to a metric-fill system of measurement several years ago. The standard bottle, whatever its shape, contains 750 milliliters of wine; this is close to a fifth of a gallon. Smaller sizes are 100 milliliters (the "miniature"); 187 milliliters (the Champagne "split"); and 375 milliliters (a half-bottle). A two-bottle container (1.5 liters) is called a Magnum if it contains Champagne or varietal wine, and a jug if it contains generic wine. Larger jug containers hold three liters, or possibly even four.

Champagne has its own sequence of bottle sizes. Knowing them is more valuable for trivia games and crossword puzzles than for use in wine shops, where the larger sizes rarely are seen. They are: split (1/2 bottle); bottle; Magnum (two bottles); Jeroboam (four bottles), Rehoboam (six bottles); Methuselah (eight bottles), Salmanazar (12 bottles), Balthazar (16 bottles), and Nebuchadnezzar (20 bottles).

Moulin-à-Vent
Appellation Contrôlée

MIS EN BOUTEILLE PAR
ROPITEAU FRÈRES
NÉGOCIANTS-ÉLEVEURS A MEURSAULT, COTE-D'OR
IMPORTED BY CHARLES LEFRANC CELLARS, SAN JOSÉ, CAL.
Sole Agent for the United States of America
ALC. 12,5 % BY VOL.   BURGUNDY WINE   750 ML   PRODUCT OF FRANCE

CORKS & CORKSCREWS

Thanks to the cork we are able to store wine and enjoy great vintages of the past. Before corks came into use, most wine was consumed near its place of origin directly from barrels that were refilled year by year as the new wine was made. Bottles stoppered with wooden plugs or rags, even if sealed with wax, did not keep wine from spoiling. Only a heavily sugared or fortified wine was able to resist oxidation and survive its youth.

The cork not only made it feasible to ship and store wine in bottles, it allowed table wines to age without spoiling. Soon after it came into use in France (the 1797 vintage of Château Lafite—now Lafite-Rothschild—holds a claim to being the first of Bordeaux's great wines to be bottled and stored for aging), wines that showed a propensity for longer life began to receive more respect and draw higher prices. Collectors could save and compare favorite wines made decades apart. For the first time, vintage years became significant and the fine wine trade was launched.

The little plug that caused this evolution is made from a tree that regenerates its bark, the *Quercus Suber,* which flourishes in Portugal. It works so well for wine because it not only possesses enough friction to stick to glass, it also has a structure, as someone put it, like "wooden moss," allowing a cork to be compressed, inserted into the bottle, and immediately spring back to its original shape. It can survive prolonged exposure to liquid without deteriorating. No other stopper can make these claims.

Corks don't just grow on trees. Bark is cut into boards, aged for a couple of years, boiled to sterilize it, and punched out in stopper shapes that are trimmed and polished. It's a costly process, so metal tops are now used for inexpensive wines. These screw tops are suitable for wines intended to be drunk young, but even modern technology cannot guarantee the same long-run protection from oxidation that corks provide. Not that corks are perfect. Sometimes they crumble or develop molds that can give a wine an off odor and an unpleasant "corky" taste. But the spoiling of wine in the bottle is not always caused by a defective cork. An imperfectly shaped bottle neck may be the culprit. Also, the human hand may neglect to store wine bottles properly. If they are not horizontal, so the wine is in contact with it, the cork will shrink over time and allow air to seep in.

In the wine world, as elsewhere, necessity is the mother of invention. Once the first wine maker stuck a cork in a bottle, the development for a tool to pull it out again was inevitable. Since that time corkscrews have been manufactured in myriad shapes and sizes and some of them have become expensive art objects.

Be wary, however: An inadequate corkscrew is sure to cause frustration and possibly embarrassment. Luckily, it's easy to separate the good from the bad. Lift up the corkscrew and look at it from the point end. If the screw (or worm) is at least two inches long and is shaped like a hollow coil, you are all right. If, however, the worm is a solid bore with a curling, sharp edge, like an auger, it will tear through a cork and not grip it properly. Suit yourself as to a corkscrew's shape and style. It's the screw that counts.

The waiter's corkscrew, which retracts the cork by lever action, is practical in a restaurant because it folds up and fits into a pocket. At home, it has no advantage over the wing-style lever opener or one that uses a two-stage counterscrew technique. One of the best corkscrews of all is the Screwpull, a space-age plastic device with a Teflon-coated, 5-inch coil screw.

Not all openers utilize a screw. Among the options, the most useful is a two-pronged metal extractor sometimes called an "Ah So." The prongs are placed between the cork and the bottle's neck and moved downward with a rocking motion. Then the cork is turned and pulled simultaneously until it emerges intact. This device is very helpful in removing weak, dried-out corks or those that have become stuck to the neck of the bottle. Having both an efficient corkscrew and an Ah So provides flexibility.

Sometimes, however, no corkscrew is equal to the task. Despite your best efforts, the cork breaks, crumbles, or does a nose dive into the bottle. What's the damage and how do you repair it?

If the cork breaks and only part comes out, you may be able to extract the remaining piece with your corkscrew or, even better at this point, an Ah So. If not, simply push it into the bottle. The cork will bob about without doing any real harm unless it jams back into the neck when you pour and causes a spill. The most prudent course is to decant the bottle.

You face more of a challenge if the cork has crumbled. Bits of cork, sometimes so tiny as to be a fine powder, will go into a glass when you pour the wine and float to the surface. To prevent this, it will be necessary to decant the wine. Pour it slowly, through several layers of cheesecloth, a tea-strainer or, if you have the patience, a coffee filter. If the debris is minimal, simply pour your portion first and all the subsequent glasses should be clear.

With champagne, the problem may be that the cork simply refuses to come out. If brute strength isn't adequate to the challenge, resort to pliers. If the top of the cork breaks off, use a corkscrew to remove the remainder, keeping your face averted from the mouth of the bottle.

The label reads:

1978

APPELLATION S.T JULIEN CONTROLÉE

Château **Gloria**
St Julien

HENRI MARTIN

PROPRIÉTAIRE A S.T JULIEN-BEYCHEVELLE

PRODUCE OF FRANCE

Mis en bouteilles au Château

RED FRENCH TABLE WINE - CONTENTS 750 ml - ALCOHOL 12 % BY VOLUME
Shipped by **DOURTHE FRÈRES, NÉGOCIANTS A BORDEAUX-GIRONDE-FRANCE**
Imported by **ALMADÉN IMPORTS,** SAN JOSÉ, CALIF.
Sole Agents for the United States of America

WINE ACCESSORIES

Once you possess the essential prerequisites for drinking wine—a bottle, a corkscrew and a glass—you are ripe to be tempted by a raft of wine-related products. As with all sports and hobbies nowadays, enterprising merchants have been alert to the opportunities to sell all manner of accessories, some of which they claim you "can't live without" and others that are unmistakably frivolous. One thing is sure: When wine becomes part of your life, you have done your relatives and friends a great favor. Not only will they share your treasured bottles with you, they will never be at a loss to find a gift for you on birthdays or holidays. You, too, will check catalogues and browse through home furnishing departments wondering if you don't need another half-dozen glasses, a new-style corkscrew, or any of the following:

High on my list are books and wine storage devices. Both are discussed in separate sections.

In the useful but not essential category, I include specialty glasses (for sherry or German white wines, for example), decanters, coasters for wine bottles, ice buckets, drip stoppers, funnels, wine cellar books for recording purchases and tasting notes, and a device for stoppering open champagne bottles.

From here on it becomes a question of the degree of your infatuation with wine and your susceptibility to temptation. Among the items waiting for your eye to fall upon them are:

Special pliers for removing champagne corks, tasting cups, devices for measuring the temperature of wine in the bottle or in the glass, decanting cradles (the expensive mechanical type is helpful when decanting heavily sedimented vintage Port), an ice stick for chilling wine in the glass, wine gift bags, and hampers designed for carrying wine to picnics or parties. The price goes up sharply for a pocket computer containing wine and vintage analyses and video wine education courses.

Wine labels and slogans appear on all manner of clothing from T-shirts and sweatshirts to hats to towels. The names or silhouettes of famous châteaux and vineyards appear on glasses, plates, and etchings. Kits provide the tools and instructions for cutting wine bottles and transforming them into lamps or other decorative objects. Name plates from the sides of wooden wine cases are transformed into laminated cheese boards or wall decorations. Photographs, drawings, and paintings of vineyards, wineries, and wine objects, some very artistic and expensive, are available. Somewhere, I suspect, there is even wallpaper featuring wine glasses or bottles.

READING ABOUT WINE

Drinking wine is rarely enough for those who are truly bitten by the wine bug. They thirst to learn more about wine, the vineyards, winemaking, to study the subject and even travel to the sites where famous wines are made. Wine education has been a rapidly growing field in this country since the 1960s. There is a Society of Wine Educators with a nationwide membership. Vineyard tours have been popular for some time, with the greatest number going to Bordeaux and Burgundy in France, along the Rhine in Germany and to the Napa Valley in California. Video cassettes offering information on tasting and vicarious tours of the vineyards have been produced as well. Several are currently on the market, with more on the way.

But, other than tastings, reading is still the primary source of wine information. There are dozens of newsletters—some with national distribution—that offer timely wine evaluations. A first-rate bi-weekly newspaper, *The Wine Spectator,* is published in San Francisco. The library of books on wine has increased dramatically over the past two decades. Although most of these books tend to go out of date as the vintages pass and new wineries and wines appear, the wine buff finds the old ones as absorbing as the new. Here is a selection of books I use often that may be helpful or agreeable to you. Some are out of print, but they turn up from time to time in bookshops that specialize in the subject.

STANDARD REFERENCE

Hugh Johnson's *Modern Encyclopedia of Wine* and Hugh Johnson's *World Atlas of Wine* (both Simon & Schuster); Alexis Lichine's *New Encyclopedia of Wines & Spirits* (Knopf); Frank Schoonmaker's *Encyclopedia of Wine* (an edition revised by Alexis Bespaloff is to be published by William Morrow in 1987); *Grossman's Guide to Wine, Beer and Spirits* by Harriet Lembeck (Scribners); *The Professional Wine Reference* by Frank E. Johnson (Harper & Row); *The Pocket Guide to Wine* by Barbara Ensrud (Putnam).

INTRODUCTORY BOOKS

Wine by Hugh Johnson (Simon & Schuster); Alexis Bespaloff's *New Signet Book of Wine* (Signet); the Wine volume of *The Good Cook* series (Time-Life Books); *Mastering Wine* by Thomas Maresca (Bantam); *Windows on the World Complete Wine Course* by Kevin Zraly (Sterling); Michael Broadbent's *Complete Guide to Wine Tasting and Wine* (Simon & Schuster).

COUNTRIES AND WINE REGIONS

The Wines of America by Leon D. Adams (McGraw-Hill); the *Signet Book of American Wines* by Peter Quimme (Signet); *Vineyards and Wineries of America* by Patrick Fegan (Stephen Greene Press); *The Book of California Wine* edited by Doris Muscatine, Bob Thompson, Maynard A. Amerine (University of California Press/Sotheby); Alexis Lichine's *Guide to the Wines and Vineyards of France* (Knopf); *Bordeaux* by Robert M. Parker Jr. (Simon & Schuster); *The Wines of the Rhône* by John Livingstone-Learmouth and Melvyn C.H. Master (Farber); *The Wines of Burgundy* by Harry W. Yoxall (Stein & Day); *The Wines of Germany* by Peter M.F. Sichel (Hastings House); *The Pocket Guide to German Wines* by Ian Jamieson (Simon & Schuster); Burton Anderson's *Guide to Italian Wines* (Simon & Schuster); *Italian Wine* by Victor Hazan (Knopf); *The Foods & Wines of Spain* by Penelope Casis (Knopf); *The Pocket Guide to Spanish Wines* by Jan Read (Simon & Schuster).

BOOKS FOR PLEASURE

On Wine by Gerald Asher (Random House); *The Fireside Book of Wine,* edited by Alexis Bespaloff (Simon & Schuster); *Burgundy* by Eunice Fried (Harper & Row); *Notes on a Cellar Book* by George Saintsbury (Macmillan); *The Great Vintage Wine Book* by Michael Broadbent (Knopf); *The Winemasters* by Nicholas Faith (Harper & Row); *The Penguin Book of Wine* by Allan Sichel (Penguin); *The Romance of Wine* by H. Warner Allen (Dutton); *Wines* by Julian Street (Knopf).

INDEX

RECIPE INDEX

CREDITS

The following were generously loaned for use in the photographs:

Page 47: English Davenport platter and Worcester
         vegetable dish—Charterhouse Antiques,
         Ltd., 115 Greenwich Avenue,
         New York City 10003
Page 49: Royal Worcester Vine Harvest dinner plate—
         Cardel, Ltd., 615 Madison Avenue,
         New York City 10022
Page 53: Antique Wedgwood plate—Trevor Potts
         Antiques, Inc., 1011 Lexington Avenue,
         New York City 10021
         Orrefors "Lisbeth" white wine glass, Kosta
         "Urica" goblet—The Royal
         Copenhagen Porcelain Company, 683
         Madison Avenue, New York City
         10021
         Vermeil flatware—Éva Jewelry & Antiques,
         1050 Second Avenue, Shop 2,
         New York City 10022
Page 63: Spoons—Éva Jewelry & Antiques
Pages 70 and 73: Dinner plates—Dorothy Hafner, 44
         Cooper Square, New York City 10003
Page 75: Sterling silver wine ewer—Charles David Ltd.,
         1050 Second Avenue, Shop 50A,
         New York City 10022
Page 76: Sterling silver ladle—Charles David Ltd.
Page 96: Victorian English Dinner plate—Charterhouse
         Antiques, Ltd.
         Knife and fork—Cardel, Ltd.